Stalking the Big Bird

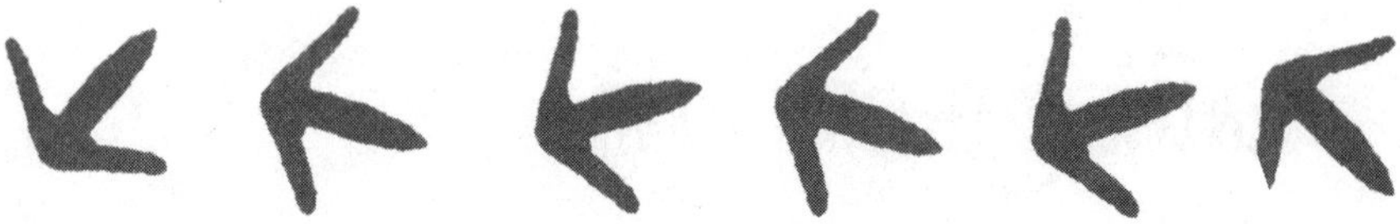

Stalking the Big Bird

A Tale of Turkeys, Biologists, and Bureaucrats

Harley G. Shaw

The University of Arizona Press
Tucson

The University of Arizona Press
© 2004 The Arizona Board of Regents
First Printing
All rights reserved

∞ This book is printed on acid-free, archival-quality paper.
Manufactured in the United States of America

09 08 07 06 05 04 6 5 4 3 2 1

Library of Congress Cataloging-in-Publication Data
Shaw, Harley G.
Stalking the big bird : a tale of turkeys, biologists, and bureaucrats /
Harley G. Shaw
p. cm.
ISBN 0-8165-2298-7 (pbk. : alk. paper)
1. Merriam's turkey. 2. Game bird management. I. Title.
QL696.G27 S49 2004
333.95'8645—dc21
2003010506

British Library Cataloguing-in-Publication Data
A catalogue record for this book is available from the British Library.

Contents

Acknowledgments

I have, perhaps, waited too long to write this book, and hence have forgotten many who were involved in the events described. Of course, Miles Rodda deserves mention here. He was my happy-go-lucky *compadre* through the entire Moqui turkey project. Even with his aches of arthritis acquired from being a cowboy in cold Montana winters, he always managed to make work fun. Don Neff shared an office with me, and we spent hours bouncing ideas back and forth. Levi Packard, the supervisor of the Arizona Game and Fish Department Region II, had a way of providing beer and an attentive ear at the end of a frustrating week. Other region II personnel—Wayne Anderson, Ray Kohls, Jack O'Neal, Harold Pratt—spent time with me in the woods and talked about turkey management. Steve Gallizioli, Ron Smith, and Ruth Betz manned the home office of the Research Division in Phoenix and tolerated my occasional frustrated outbursts. They did more to help the project along than I would have been willing to acknowledge at the time. Ron should have had his name on any paper or report that resulted from the study. I only realized this later. Mountain Bell employees Anon Willis and Ed Comstock spent hours helping me learn a little about electronics—knowledge I quickly shed as soon as Dave Beaty and his telemetry equipment came on the scene. Fred Phillips became an icon in turkey management and is given his due in the book. In our later efforts, Ron Day and Jim Wegge handled much of the trapping during the transition period, when Brian Wakeling was taking over turkey research. More recently, studies by Brian, Cheryl Mollohan, Mark Rumble in South Dakota, and Rick Hoffman in Colorado have increased our understanding of turkey habitat immensely. Karen Mock has clarified the genetic relationships of subspecies. Much of their work is only now being assimilated into the management lore of agencies.

Preface

The core subject of this book is the Merriam's wild turkey, the sub-species of turkey native to the southern Rocky Mountains and the Colorado Plateau. However, the book's purpose is not necessarily to teach turkey biology but rather to demonstrate the difficulties of gaining and implementing new knowledge of a single wild species (or a single subspecies as is the case here). I think anyone confused over the complexities of modern wildlife conservation might find this book of interest. Since the publication of Aldo Leopold's *Game Management* in 1933, along with the passage of the Pittman-Robertson Act in 1937, state and federal wildlife agencies have functioned under the belief that increased knowledge produced by research would improve our ability to manage wildlife. We must hope that this is true, but the information that follows herein suggests that the more we know about a species and the system within which it lives, the more difficult clear decisions may become. In fact, ignorance and decisiveness can be very compatible bedmates.

I have become concerned that humans lack the wisdom needed to manage wildlife, even if all we have to do is apply biological fact. Given the complexities created by multiple human desires, the management of wildlife begins to look hopeless. What people want is rarely, perhaps never, derived from any understanding of ecology. In fact, more often than not, we develop myths that sound like science to justify our wants. If we add one other complicating element—the fact that management to favor one desired wildlife species is likely to be antagonistic to the needs of other, often also desired species—rational wildlife management begins to look impossible.

The process of single species management, rather than turkeys, is therefore the real subject of this book. Merriam's turkeys are the object around which I built the manuscript, simply because they happen to be a creature that I studied. Any other wildlife species would probably serve as well. The book is more of a personal essay than a factual discourse. It is an effort to describe, from the perspective of a field biologist working on a single subspecies, the complexities of modern, politicized wildlife science. Some things, such as the internal politics of an agency, can only be described from my own narrow and prejudiced viewpoint, and others may remember these things differently. If I had a consistent problem as an employee of a government agency, it lay in my assumptions that everyone shared my perspectives, which I often unthinkingly considered to be obvious truths. Working away from the central offices of the agency, I usually blundered ahead under such assumptions until I was caught up short, quite often blindsided unexpectedly, and I reacted quite often with anger and frustration.

So, if my discussion is not completely fair to everyone, so be it. Where I'm critical, I won't provide names. I write about the events to show that such conflicts are a part of the process, not to castigate individuals. The events are long enough past to be unimportant in my present life, and I can now view them with more humor than anger. And of course, I was entirely capable of making mistakes on my own. My own bumbling over the years, trying to force a little more information out of some uncooperative species, could be the subject of a potboiler, if anyone wanted to take me to task. So, when I criticize the system, I do so from the insecure bastions of my own glass house. I was part of that system, so I'll also tell a few stories on myself, just to keep someone else from getting the first shot. Of course, there are some stories I probably will never tell; and there may be mistakes I never knew I made. Perhaps the confessionals here will add a little humor to temper the frustrations.

In writing about the actual research, I present the scientific premises upon which turkey biology is based, along with some of our research results. As the amount of information available on any wild species increases, our view of that species becomes increasingly complex, and the volume of information unmanageable. I have chosen not to formally cite scientific literature. Where appropriate, I will discuss specific references and authors in the text. For anyone seeking detailed knowledge of wild turkeys, I recommend the National Wild Turkey Federation's fine book, *The Wild Turkey: Biology and Management,* edited by James G. Dickson and published in 1992. For a scholarly treatment of the history of human interactions with the wild turkey, I recommend A. W. Schorger's 1966 book, *The Wild Turkey: Its History and Domestication.* A list of additional suggested readings is provided at the end of this book.

Stalking the Big Bird

1 Salting Tails

My interest in catching birds goes back quite a ways. I remember trying to catch a rooster when I was about four on my grandparents' farm on the South Canadian River in Oklahoma. I spent hours chasing the squawking fowl with no success. Finally one of my teenaged uncles told me, "Boy, if you'll put salt on that chicken's tail, you'll be able to catch him." I hate to admit it, but I think I actually did borrow my grandmother's salt shaker for a short time. But even at that age, I finally realized that if I could get close enough to salt the rooster's tail, I could grab it, salt or no. I never did catch the rooster, but I was much more wary of any instructions handed out by my Oklahoma relatives after that.

I remembered this incident when I began to try to capture and mark Merriam's turkeys as a research biologist for the Arizona Game and Fish Department. We experimented with two types of traps that other biologists had used elsewhere. One of these was a wooden cage with a drop gate that triggered when the turkey entered the trap. After a couple of months running a line of several of these traps, I began to feel as if I was driving around the woods with my grandmother's salt shaker in hand. I finally caught one hen turkey and my own Brittany spaniel before deciding to put greater effort into the second trap, which was called a cannon net.

My first effort with a cannon net occurred in late summer, 1966, near Fort Valley, just northwest of Flagstaff. It involved three mature gobblers that Miles Rodda and I had attracted to bait. Miles, my partner on the project, was an aspiring western artist who had grown up on a ranch in Montana. In fact, he ultimately inherited the ranch. But he found more satisfaction in sketching the bighorns that he could see from his front porch than from fixing fence or throwing hay during long Montana winters. Those winters, in fact, had given him arthritis at an early age, and Arizona's sunshine, combined with the success of several southwestern wildlife artists, had attracted the young rancher. By the time he left the ranch, Miles had six children. Income supplanting his painting quickly became essential. His outdoor skills were attractive to us, and working with wildlife fit into his artistic ambitions. We hired him, with about 50 percent of his time to be spent working with me on turkeys.

After attempting to bait turkeys at several locations, we finally had birds daily visiting our oats at one site, although the time of their visits was unpredictable. We set the cannon net as best we knew how, cautiously adding nets, wire, and cannons, and built a blind, one piece at a time, one day at a time. We did not want to frighten the birds. A week passed before we were ready to try a shot.

We entered our burlap blind one fall morning before sunup, then sat immobile for six hours, waiting for the birds to arrive. They finally appeared at the edge of the small forest clearing and fed leisurely to an appropriate position in front of the net. We flipped the switch to fire the cannons. Nothing happened. We checked the wires and flipped the switch again. Nothing. The birds leisurely pecked at the remaining grain, keeping us pinned down in the blind for another hour, then drifted away into the ponderosa pine forest. After checking our wiring, we concluded that the six-volt dry cell provided with the net wasn't producing enough current to ignite the small explosive black-powder squibs that fired the cannons.

The next day we were back with a twelve-volt auto battery, charged and tested. Lack of spark would never again be a problem with the cannon net. Once more, the birds eventually arrived, but one of the gobblers had become suspicious. He refused to feed in front of the net. The other two approached the bait nervously. We began to fear that the anxious pacing of the uncooperative bird would frighten the two in front of the net. We had the feeling that the entire game department was watching and waiting for us to catch turkeys, so we badly wanted to report birds in hand. We flipped the switch, and the cannons roared with fire and smoke. The net shot upward at about forty-five degrees, hit its apex, and hung in the air for what seemed like minutes (more likely microseconds). The two birds in front of the net flushed and easily escaped before it descended. Amazingly, the one wary tom also flushed, following the other two birds, and was directly under the net as it came down.

That evening, we shared a six-pack of beer in reserved celebration. We had caught our first bird, but we knew our net had been set badly, and that a single turkey was now sporting a colored back tag as the result of pure beginners' luck. With all the wisdom that hindsight provides, we decided to try a few experimental shots before returning to the field. We had not done this earlier, because our budget was small, equipment was limited, and setting and untangling the cannon net was a lot of work. We had wanted every shot to provide turkeys. But experimentation was obviously needed.

Our setup in a field near home mimicked the one that had failed so successfully. A couple of neighbors came to watch the fireworks. We once more produced the smoke, fire, and noise. The net sailed as it had in the woods, following two of the projectiles over a single phone line that we had judged to be above our line of fire. We spent the rest of the day gingerly trying to get the net down without breaking the fragile line. At this point, we wisely concluded that we were setting the cannons at too high an angle. With a couple more shots the next day, we developed a low arc that fairly slammed the net to the ground. We were ready to go back to the woods.

One year earlier, I had asked to be assigned to this new turkey study. I had been working on a mule deer project that, while interesting enough, required me to live in Phoenix. One of the reasons I had chosen wildlife as a profession was my dislike of cities. The turkey study would allow me to move to Flagstaff, a smaller community in the high country of Arizona. It would also allow me to live closer to my area of research and do my fieldwork with less time away from home.

The main objective of the turkey project was a long-discussed evaluation of the effects of fall hunting on turkey numbers. Arizona had never held a spring hunt for turkeys. Spring hunting, wherein breeding males, called gobblers or toms, are lured by camouflaged hunters making henlike noises, was a traditional practice in the south-eastern United States. For some reason, Arizona had always treated turkeys as a big game species. Turkey hunts had occurred in the fall, along with other hunting seasons, and a center-fire rifle was required to shoot them. Since the 1940s, this fall hunt had been closely regu-lated, with only a few permits allocated each year to hunters lucky enough to be drawn during a late summer lottery.

The proposed study reflected the Arizona Game and Fish De-partment's desire to eliminate the lottery system for allocating per-mits, allowing anyone to buy a turkey tag and hunt during the two-week season. At the time, a move was afoot to simplify regulations. If they had no obvious biological purpose, eliminating the expense and inconvenience of drawings made sense.[1] The need for such restricted hunting had been challenged by studies of Gambel's quail in south-ern Arizona that had demonstrated that fall hunting had virtually no effect on quail populations.

Turkeys, like quail, produce large broods during summer and often experience relatively high natural losses during winter. Fall hunt-ing is based on the premise that many of the birds taken by hunters would die anyway during the winter. Their mortality is merely shifted from natural causes to the hunter's gun. Within reasonable hunting levels, the number of birds surviving until spring will remain the same with or without hunting. The movement to more liberal forms of tur-key hunting was thus an extrapolation from the quail research, but declines in turkey numbers that had occurred earlier in the century made wildlife administrators cautious. At least initially, they wanted to test the ability of some smaller population of turkeys to withstand greater hunting pressure before they liberalized regulations statewide.

What the Arizona Game and Fish Department had in mind for the study, I believe, was three to four years of intensive monitoring of a turkey population under a hunting regime that allowed anyone to hunt over a two-week season. As a young scientist fresh out of grad school and steeped in statistics, however, I envisioned a more rigorous design. I recommended that we establish a treated (hunted) area and a control (nonhunted) area, to lessen the possibility that any population variations we saw were simply natural fluctuations. After five years, I would reverse the treatments, hunting the previously nonhunted area and closing the other unit to hunting. This followed accepted research protocol and emulated the earlier quail research.[2]

When I approached the department's administration with two management units I thought suitable for the project, they refused to close either area to hunting. I hadn't considered extra demands on law enforcement personnel, nor had I recognized that each of these units was the preferred hunting ground of a particular community or group of hunters. These hunters would raise holy hell if their favorite hunting areas were closed. Hence, the agency that had assigned the study now turned down the design I felt was needed to accomplish it. I was befuddled, but I adjusted my thinking and substituted an area, popularly called the Moqui, in the Kaibab National Forest just south of the Grand Canyon. I stubbornly hoped to use the turkey habitat in the National Forest as a hunted area and the adjacent area within Grand Canyon National Park as an unhunted control. This eliminated any chance for reversal of units in the experiment, but it created an illusion of proper scientific design. I assumed that the bulk of the fall take by hunters would be young birds of the year, just as it was in quail. If the hypothesis was right, hunter success should vary directly with the percentage of young birds in the late summer population, and the population, as measured early each fall, would not be affected by hunting.

I planned to use two census methods to monitor the turkey populations. One of these was intensive, late-summer roadside surveying, meant to detect yearly changes in turkey numbers and to estimate the success of the annual hatch of young turkeys. In doing these roadside surveys, a crew of biologists from the department drove the same selected back roads during the early fall each year and counted and classified all turkeys seen. We also marked the exact location where we saw them. Routes on the Moqui study were fifteen miles in length.

They were driven morning and evening for five days, for a total of ten passes over each route.

The second census technique was a capture-recapture method. This method, using hunter returns of marked birds as well as marked birds sighted on annual surveys, would yield a second estimate of actual fall turkey numbers, as well as an estimate of the proportion of the turkey population killed by hunters. This is a highly researched method used in wildlife population studies. With knowledge of the number of birds we had marked, we could use a ratio to estimate the actual total turkey population on the area. This method requires, however, that a fairly high proportion of total birds be marked and that surveys occur fairly quickly after marking. We could never satisfy this requirement on the Moqui study. It was dependent upon our ability to mark young turkeys during the late summer—something, as it turned out, we never succeeded in doing.

In 1965, we did not yet have miniature radios to use in following the birds. We had only colored tags of various designs. Color marking had a variety of uses. We hoped that the individual birds wearing highly-visible plastic streamers in the center of their backs could be identified afield, allowing us to study daily and seasonal movements, death rates, cause of death, and, perhaps, to begin to learn something about turkey social behavior.

To fit birds with markers of any kind, we had, of course, to catch them. This had seemed a simple matter. Wild turkeys had long been trapped by Indians and by early settlers with crude pole traps built from materials in the forest. Remains of some of these traps were still visible when early wildlife biologists first arrived in the southwestern woods. But such primitive traps didn't serve our purposes. Our work would cover large areas, and we needed to be mobile. Also, we were uneasy about leaving assembled traps in the woods between trapping periods for fear of vandalism or misuse by poachers.

Besides, better methods existed. The cannon net described earlier had been developed by waterfowl biologists by the 1950s. And although we did not, at first, have great success with this method, it did have the potential of catching fifteen to twenty birds in a single shot. Eastern turkey biologists had quickly adapted it to their needs for marking or transplanting birds. The tool had already been used in Arizona in transplanting turkeys. Also, in New Mexico, biologists had developed a portable version of the pole trap, made from wooden panels. It could be carried in the back of a pickup and assembled at the trapping site. We would use both methods before we were finished.

But however well developed the technology, catching turkeys requires some level of skill, experience, and perseverance. To begin, you must know something about the behavior of the bird, and, as we eventually learned, some folks are naturally better suited to the task than others. It takes an immense amount of patience. I decided early that I am among those who are not by nature turkey trappers, even though I've caught my share of the birds. It's a form of work I dread. Sitting motionless in blinds or cramped pickup seats and waiting for turkeys to appear on the bait is not my notion of fun. It loses more glamour when the temperature is hovering near zero. But then I don't suppose the birds, when caught, enjoy it either.

Location of sites and dispersal of bait is a skill of its own. Even after you learn to attract the birds, the cannon net, and its successor, the rocket net, provide a large variety of opportunities for mistakes. An eye for detail is necessary—as we had discovered on our first effort.

2 Soaring with Turkeys

I eventually realized that the South Rim of the Grand Canyon was a poor choice for a study site. The area of turkey habitat within the National Park was too small. Turkeys used it mainly in the summer and fall and ranged regularly onto the National Forest, where turkeys were hunted. There was no separation between the hunted and nonhunted populations. Also, as our check station results demonstrated, the South Rim was too far from major human population centers to attract enough hunters to test fall hunting effects adequately. Even without the restriction of specially drawn permits, hunting pressure on the area remained relatively low.

As events proceeded, the suitability of the area for the study became moot. Within a year after we began to gather data, the Arizona Game and Fish Commission, the governor-appointed citizen's committee that establishes hunting regulations, eliminated the requirements for fall turkey hunting permits and opened a spring hunt in our study area. This action implied that the Commission felt no need for the study and was moving on without waiting for the research results. It left me feeling rather useless and a bit betrayed. I broached this seeming contradiction at a meeting between the game management and research branches of the Game and Fish Department. Both branch chiefs and various supervisors were present, as were field biologists from both divisions. The meeting was a periodic event intended to allow research biologists to communicate their findings to the management side of the department, thereby speeding implementation of new information. It also allowed the wildlife management personnel to make suggestions regarding research. I hoped that someone in this group could explain the turn of events in turkey management and, perhaps, renew my conviction that I was still doing something worthwhile.

My presentation came late in the day, and I dutifully described my objectives and procedures. The study was as yet too young to yield results. At the end of my presentation, I asked for questions. There were few, if any. So I gathered my courage (I was still young, shy, and naive) and stated that I would like to ask something. Everyone listened politely. "Can anyone," I blurted, "tell me why the hell we're doing this study?"

The branch chiefs looked at each other and shrugged. Their underlings looked shocked or embarrassed. Finally, one chief answered tentatively, "Well, as best I can remember, we held a meeting about five years ago to develop a list of research priorities. This one was on it, and it finally came to the top."

I stumbled back to my seat in shock. If there was no more than this to selection of projects, and if the agency was willing to waste both the years of my life and license buyers' money, what was I doing here? My shock converted into a quiet rage over the next week or so. I brooded, then finally wrote a brief note to my supervisor suggesting that, because of the Commission's action, the study had become a bit of a white elephant. I received a curt reply pointing out that I was the one who had asked to be assigned to turkey research, and that he was concerned about my attitude. I brooded several more days, then scribbled a fiery, six-page, handwritten letter on legal-sized paper, spelling out the problem as I saw it. In this letter, I suggested that habitat modifications due to logging or grazing might be greater threats to turkey populations than hunting and were perhaps better candidates for research. The week after I submitted these comments, I was camped out on a javelina project and, because of the critical tone of my letter, I daily expected a radio call telling me to bring my equipment to Phoenix and find a new job. But no such call came.

I had to pass through Phoenix on my way home, so I stopped at the office and humbly placed myself in front of my supervisor's desk, expecting at the very least a good scolding. He gave me a mysterious smile and began to ask questions about the previous week's work. The discussion then went to recent fishing trips, quail hunting, and the health of my family. Finally, another division chief stuck his head in the door, noticed my presence, and asked congenially, "How's the turkey work going?" Before I could speak, my supervisor stated, "We're planning some major changes in that project." No other details were discussed that day. As I left, my supervisor said, "Write up what you think we should be doing."

I realized, as I drove to my home in Flagstaff, that a quiet discussion on the subject in my supervisor's office, rather than a challenge in a meeting, would have been a better way to broach the problem. Over the next few days, I began to write a proposal for studies of turkey habitat. In the short time that I had worked on the bird, I had begun to see that good information on habitat requirements was clearly needed and that such information would allow us to begin to assess the effects of other land use activities, especially logging, on turkey numbers. I felt that such studies would have long-term value, if we could accomplish them.

While I was working on the habitat study plans, Miles and I continued our efforts to trap birds. The hunter effects study continued, with the understanding that the data gathered there might be used for habitat research as well. Whatever our study objectives, we needed basic information on seasonal movements of turkeys. Also, we needed to continue to improve our trapping skills. We caught turkeys, but not without new and varied difficulties. The cannon net and its successor, the rocket net, are fraught with potential problems that can be exacerbated by inattentive operators. With these tools, Murphy's law is in full force. Once, for example, we forgot to attach the cannon projectiles to the net. These are heavy metal tubes, weighing five to ten pounds apiece. The net we were using had four of these that were supposed to be tied along the leading edge of the folded net. They pulled the net through the air, looping it over feeding birds, when the cannon was fired. Luckily, birds did not come to bait that day. Had we fired, we might still be searching down range for the projectiles.

Another time, we had been persuaded to try a supposedly new

and improved powder for the old cannon net. This new compound arrived while we were baiting birds, with detailed directions and full assurance that it was better and safer than black powder. We loaded it, birds came to bait, we fired, and the projectiles barely left their bases, flopping harmlessly among the feeding birds. The net didn't move, and the turkeys didn't even spook badly. They let out inquisitive "purrrts" and walked away stiff-necked, seemingly wondering what the hell that was all about. We went back to black powder.

Once we somehow wired the detonators improperly. This was not a job that required an electronics degree. You simply attached the two wires from the black powder squibs to two wires running to the battery in the blind. But this day we had a new assistant who claimed to have blasting experience. While Miles and I saw to the details of net folding, projectile attachment, and camouflage (all items now on a checklist), the new man wired the charges. As a supervisor, I've always made the error of assuming everyone knows more than I do, especially if they tell me they do. I didn't check on him.

Black powder squibs come from the factory with the loose ends of their wires wound together. When we armed the cannons, we had to separate the squib wires and attach them to a pair of larger wires running into the blind. We fired the cannons by tapping the other ends of these wires on the posts of a well-charged auto battery. I had glanced at the wiring before entering the blind, but only to see if everything was camouflaged. The fact that the wires *were* well covered actually prevented me from inspecting the connections. We crawled into the hidden tent and settled for the usual indeterminate wait. Within a half hour after daybreak, birds were on bait. They soon were in position and Miles whispered "fire." The new assistant was near the battery and touched the wires to the posts. I was in the back of the blind, where I couldn't see, but the sound of the detonating cannons caused my jaw to drop. Instead of the expected loud "whoom" of the synchronized explosions, I heard a sequential "boom, boom, boom, boom" with a distinct interval between each explosion. Miles, who had been watching the net, threw his hands up in exasperation. I said, somewhat dazedly, "You know that isn't possible, don't you?"

It goes without saying that all the turkeys left the scene. We crawled from the blind to assess the problem. Instead of being spread like a blanket over a flock of flailing birds, the net was stretched and twisted. Projectiles, ropes, and wires were wound and tangled in one big linear gob. We spent the rest of the day getting it unwound and properly folded. We discovered that the new man had not separated the wires, but rather had twisted connected strands around a single lead from the blind. I'm surprised that the squibs fired at all. They probably wouldn't have if we hadn't had the powerful spark provided by the freshly charged auto battery.[1]

Our most serious error involved placing our blind fifty yards downrange from the cannons. At this site, it seemed to be the only angle that gave us a view of the baited net. We manned this blind before sunup on a cold, damp morning following several days of snow. We had cleared heavy snow from the net before entering the blind, but failed to notice that thawing midday temperatures had soaked through the strip of canvas we used to cover the net. This canvas lay loosely over the folded net, allowing us to cover it with forest litter as camouflage. Normally, the net flowed smoothly out from under the canvas when the cannons were fired. But this time, the net was a wet, rigid lump, frozen solid. When birds were in position, we fired. The net stayed put, and three of the four rockets hit the ends of their ropes and slammed to the ground, sending startled birds in every direction. But the rope of the fourth projectile broke, and suddenly some ten pounds of hard, cold steel was arching through the early morning sky. The light tent we used as a blind did not allow upward vision, and it seemed horribly inadequate as a bomb shelter. There was no time to run and no place to go. The two of us hunkered down, then heard a metallic clank in the rocks beyond us. Needless to say, we always checked for frozen nets after that, and we positioned our blind away from any potential impact area.

I could tell a few more stories, but I think this explains projectile nets. When they work, you catch turkeys. If you screw up, anything can happen.

3 The Object of Our Obsession

Before I get further into our activities as Merriam's turkey students, perhaps some definition of the object of our research is in order. What is a Merriam's turkey? What makes it different than other wild turkeys? Who says? Why does it matter?

I'll tackle the last question first. As we have learned more about habitat requirements and factors influencing habitat selection, the concept of subspecies has taken on greater significance in wildlife management. Merriam's wild turkey is the subspecies native to the forests of Arizona, New Mexico, and Colorado. A subspecies in zoology is approximately equivalent to the category of race in humans. In modern wildlife management, the notion of nativeness gives creatures special status. It makes sense to protect the habitat of native wildlife, which can then be expected to thrive where they evolved without excessive help from humans. Among many modern wildlife biologists, creatures living where they evolved are considered ecologically pure, while those transplanted by humans are seen as quasi-domestic and tainted. This makes sense as long as you know all there is to know about the origins of a species. However, when you get down to individual species or subspecies, such a puritanical viewpoint may have faults. The very concept of nativeness is vague, and the term "native" and even its more snobbish synonym, "indigenous," lose resolution upon scrutiny.

Nativeness is dependent to some extent on human perceptions. It properly refers to species that have resided for millennia in given regions (which also slowly move, by the way, according to the concepts of continental drift). It may also be applied to species with obscure histories that just happened to be in a particular place when naturalists first arrived to discover them. Rearrangement of plants and animals over time, with or without human help, has been so common that nativeness may become moot in the longer time frame of geology. At the time a species is first acknowledged by authorities, its origins may not be obvious. Its presumed nativeness therefore signifies certain tenure, but not necessarily roots. Times and modes of species arrival are uncertainties that we have only recently begun to study. And many uncertainties exist.

Such is the case with the Merriam's wild turkey. The wild turkey is certainly native to the North American continent. Remains of *Meleagris gallopavo,* a modern species of turkey, have been found in southeastern United States and Mexico in Pleistocene deposits (one million to twelve thousand years ago), so turkeys resided in these areas prior to the arrival of humans (currently estimated to be no more than twelve thousand years ago). However, although wild turkeys were present in Arizona, New Mexico, and Colorado—the historic range of the Merriam's turkey—when the first Spaniards arrived in the 1500s, no fossil evidence exists as yet suggesting that they preceded earlier human occupation of the region.

During the 250 years following Spanish exploration of the Southwest, hunters and naturalists noticed color differences across the range of the turkey and ultimately classified six separate subspecies to account for these differences. The Merriam's turkey was recognized as a subspecies unique to Arizona, Colorado, and New Mexico. In modern classification systems, a subspecies is usually considered to have evolved within the area to which it is native. Its differences are assumed to be adaptations to its habitat. As we shall see later, some people question the native southwestern origins of the Merriam's turkey.

The turkey can, of course, easily be accepted as a species separate from other birds. There's nothing else like it, and its classification at this level requires no extraordinary justification. Discussion of its classification could end here, if our subject was turkeys in general. But, as already mentioned, we assume that southwestern turkeys are unique and we call them Merriam's turkeys. What has brought about this special status, and is it valid?

Many books have been written about the criteria used to distinguish species and more on the philosophies that underlie the criteria. The specialties of systematic biology and taxonomy deal respectively with evolved relationships of extinct and living creatures and with the proper naming of these creatures. These are mature sciences that traditionally compare size, shape, color, behavior, and geographic distribution of organisms. Specialists within these disciplines are now incorporating the studies of DNA into their older classifications, thereby probing the very cellular mechanisms that cause living things to diversify. As a result, classification systems are changing. New knowledge is forging ahead of old systems, and some of the categories we use, including subspecies, may someday become obsolete. Their definitions will certainly change.

The species is the smallest discrete subdivision that biologists recognize in their efforts to classify life forms on earth. Subspecies are used to acknowledge shades of variation within this discrete category. One simple criterion for differentiating the two categories says that given the chance, different species will not interbreed, but subspecies within a species may. Subspecific classification is a way of acknowledging subtle size, shape, or color differences across the geographic range of a species. Very often a subspecies designation does little more than recognize that a species lives in varying habitats and therefore must have evolved a range of physical differences.[1]

In early classifications, these differences often seemed to exist only in the eye of the naturalist bestowing the subspecies its name. In the 1700s and 1800s, classification was the main occupation of field biologists. These early scientists were trying to describe and name what they observed as they explored new regions, but their legacy has taken on new meaning over time. Trophy hunters, for example, may now travel widely to shoot one of each subspecies of turkey (or bighorn sheep, or elk, or white-tailed deer), calling such accomplishments "grand slams." Bird watchers tally life lists that value equally sightings of subspecies and species. And most important, environmental law, especially the Endangered Species Act, has given taxonomy a renewed significance, and some endangered subspecies have become banners in battles to preserve habitat. Industries based on natural resources are finding their plans increasingly stymied by laws protecting some relatively obscure creature. Land developers, loggers, ranchers, and lawyers have suddenly become brutally aware of the subtleties of biological classification.

But back to turkeys. Only two species of living turkeys are known to exist. The ocellated turkey, *Agriocharis oscellata,* is native to the lowlands of southeast Mexico, Guatemala, and Belize. The North American wild turkey (including the domestic turkey) has the scientific name *Meleagris gallopavo,* a name with a convoluted history that I will briefly summarize here. Anyone interested in more detailed coverage should refer to A. W. Schorger's book, *The Wild Turkey.*

When specimens of New World animals and plants began to arrive in Europe with the first expeditions returning from the Americas, sixteenth-century naturalists had a heyday. But the early mariners weren't naturalists, and their record keeping was not always the best. For nearly a century, no one in Europe seemed to be sure whether turkeys came from America, India, or Africa. In 1533, forty years after Christopher Columbus returned from his first voyage, an Italian naturalist called the bird *Gallo peregrino.* This might be loosely interpreted as "wandering chicken," perhaps reflecting the confusion regarding its origin. In 1555, a French naturalist, Pierre Belon, attached the name *Meleagris,* the Greek name for guinea, which is an African fowl. Use of this name also may reflect confusion over origins of the bird, or perhaps over the location of the Americas.

Gallopavo was suggested as the name for the turkey about 1677. This name combines the genera of the chicken or African cock (*Gallus*) and the Indian or south Asian peafowl (*Pavo*), and reflects the turkey's similarities to both of these. Whoever suggested the name may have even considered it a cross between the two. *Gallopavo* was still being used for the genus of the bird as late as 1760. By this time, Carolus Linneaus took things in hand and decided that *Meleagris* deserved historic priority and made it the genus of the turkey. In the tenth edition of his *Systema Naturae* (1758), *gallopavo* was used as the specific designation. Even though other names were subsequently suggested, the turkey has officially been *Meleagris gallopavo* for well over two hundred years. Odds are the name will stick.

At present, the Merriam's turkey is one of six subspecies of *Meleagris gallopavo:* the Eastern Wild turkey (*M. g. sylvestris*); the Florida turkey (*M. g. osceola*); the Rio Grande turkey (*M. g. intermedia*); the Merriam's turkey (*M. g. merriami*); the Gould's turkey (*M. g. mexicana*); and the South Mexican turkey (*M. g. gallopavo*). Note that no clear relationship exists between common and scientific names for all the subspecies, but our subject, *M. g. merriami,* is called Merriam's turkey, which seems perfectly reasonable.

Based on A. W. Schorger's review of the history of turkeys in the southwest, early Spanish explorers were fascinated with the domestic turkeys they found among the Indians, but were amazingly silent regarding the presence of wild turkeys. Father Luis Velarde apparently made the first mention by Spaniards of wild turkeys in Arizona in 1716, long after the trips of Francisco Vásquez de Coronado and Fra Marcos de Niza. Antonio Barreiro noted wild turkeys in New Mexico in 1832.

Anglo explorers seemed to be more interested in the wild bird, and G. C. Sibley, as early as 1825, mentioned that the turkeys in New Mexico were colored differently than those along the Missouri River. Mountain man and guide Antoine Leroux pointed out the differences to the naturalist Samuel Woodhouse in 1851. By the mid-1800s, quite a few folks were aware that the turkeys of Arizona, New Mexico, and Colorado had more white in their feathers than birds further east. After being briefly designated as a separate species, the southwestern turkey was finally established as the subspecies *merriami* in 1900 by the American taxonomist, Edward Nelson, to honor the American naturalist C. Hart Merriam. Merriam is known for developing the life zone system of plant community classification, an inspiration resulting from his 1890s expedition to the San Francisco Peaks in the heart of Merriam's turkey country.

The Gould's turkey, however, has the subspecific name of *mexicana* after the country that encompasses most of its range. The original specimen was actually named *Meleagris mexicana* in 1856 by British ornithologist and artist John Gould, who considered it a new and separate species. Later taxonomists revised it to *M. g. mexicana.* Although its subspecies is now *mexicana,* it is still popularly called Gould's turkey, since John Gould originally named it.[2]

So far, the common names applied to the subspecies make sense, even if the relationships between common and scientific names seem inconsistent. But we can raise the level of confusion. The subspecies native to southeastern Mexico, called appropriately the South Mexican turkey, is named *Meleagris gallopavo gallopavo.* Use of *gallopavo* twice suggests that this is the subspecies from which original (or type) specimens for the species were collected, nothing more. It does not necessarily signify anything about evolutionary timing of the subspecies. *M. g. gallopavo* came from the area where the early Spanish ships landed and probably represents the first form of turkey taken home and seen by Belon, Linneaus, and the other European naturalists. What they first classified may have been domestic birds acquired from native peoples.[3] The common name, South Mexican, reflects its range, but it does not relate in any way to its subspecific title.

M. g. sylvestris is called the Eastern turkey, because it occurs in the eastern half of the United States. *Sylvestris* refers to forests or trees, and we might call this bird the forest turkey, if we were to try to associate common and scientific name. But Eastern it is, and this works okay as long as we stay within the U.S. borders, where East and West are separated by the Great Plains. From Tokyo, Eastern turkey range lies a long way to the west.

The Rio Grande turkey is also named popularly for its range, typically from a narrow *norteamericano* perspective. While the bird certainly exists along the Rio Grande, most of its range is in Mexico, well away from that river. Its scientific name is *M. g. intermedia,* the intermediate turkey. This fits. The bird is intermediate in color between the dark eastern bird and the lighter Merriam's, Gould's, or South Mexican turkeys. It also ranges geographically between the eastern and southwestern subspecies.

Finally the Florida turkey, a small, dark subspecies existing only in Florida, is named *M. g. osceola*. Osceola was a Seminole chief, who had nothing to do, insofar as I can determine, with turkey taxonomy.

Thus the current system of naming turkeys developed over a period of almost four hundred years, starting when the early Spanish ships brought birds back to Europe and ending with Nelson's delineation of the Merriam's turkey in 1900. This classification of southwestern turkeys is still occasionally disputed. As late as 1938, a biologist attempted to add another Mexican subspecies, *M. g. onusta,* but proper authorities did not accept it. For the present, a system with six subspecies, with three in the southwestern United States, prevails.

Common names, such as Eastern turkey or Merriam's turkey, develop locally over time and are accepted by popular consensus. In fact, various localities and regions within the range of the wild turkey often develop their own names, and will not recognize the common names we have used here. Scientific nomenclature is equally complex, but it is at least governed by the International Ornithologist's Union. Their rules give weight to prior use of names, appropriateness, and adequacy of description, but the rules may be overridden, if an old name is so well established that it is unlikely to change. Scientific names, too, can therefore display the influence of human whim and fancy.

In general, the differences between turkey subspecies are based on color, with western birds having more white in their feathers than those further east. Some size differences also exist, but these overlap considerably and do not serve well in separation of the regional differences. The two dark eastern subspecies (*sylvestris* and *osceola*) are visibly different than birds further west.[4]

Distinguishing between the Rio Grande, Merriam's, and the two Mexican turkeys on a practical level is more difficult. Distinguishing free-ranging Merriam's from Gould's or South Mexican turkeys on the basis of color is, I believe, questionable. The subtleties of color separating them in written descriptions, mainly faint differences in "pinkish" or "buff" shadings in the white feathers, are impossible to see on free-ranging wild birds. They are of dubious value even with birds in hand. As late as 1983, for example, southwestern ornithologist Amadeo Rea attempted to narrow the distinction between Gould's and Merriam's turkeys. He noted: "A study of both Gould's and Merriam's Turkeys in our collection and at the University of Arizona showed that the well-publicized characters separating these two races were completely inconstant." He then went on to describe one characteristic, the ratio of the width of the blue band on the rump feathers, that seemed to differentiate these subspecies. This work has not, as far as I can determine, been published in a technical journal, and exact details of how this ratio is measured are not available. But even if the characteristic is valid, it would not help one to identify free-ranging birds. Considering the amount of variation in coloration that occurs within wild populations of turkeys, I remain skeptical of subspecific classifications based upon slight feather color distinctions.

Measurement of body, particularly bone and skull, characteristics is a common tool in taxonomy and would seem to be a better method for determining subspecific differences. But here again problems exist. Historically, sample sizes available for some subspecies are small, and ranges of measurements overlap. In the most recent evaluation of turkey nomenclature, based on bone and feather measurements, taxonomist Peter Stangel and his coworkers at the University of Alabama concluded that variation within subspecies was too great to clearly distinguish between them. The Gould's turkey is the largest, with Merriam's and South Mexican ranking close together at second and third. But measurements alone could not consistently separate Merriam's and South Mexican from the Eastern or Rio Grande. The Florida turkey alone was distinct in its consistently small size.

Weights and beard lengths also failed to separate subspecies, although the small size of the Florida turkey again distinguished it. Shorter spur length of males separated Gould's from all other subspecies, and seemed to separate southwestern turkeys from all eastern subspecies. The South Mexican turkey, however, was not included in the analysis of weight, beard length, or spur length. The authors doing this assessment emphasized the inadequacy of current data on turkey taxonomy and called for additional study of bone shape and molecular genetics.

A few archaeologists, perhaps because they are accustomed to working with incomplete specimens, tend to be bolder in their assignment of specimens to subspecies. Charmion McKusick of Globe, Arizona, believes that she can distinguish between Merriam's, Gould's, and at least two forms of ancient domestic turkeys. She finds it more difficult to separate the Merriam's from the Eastern turkey. Her methodology, largely based on differences in size and shape of leg bones, has not been incorporated into the mainstream of turkey systematics.

As ornithologists learn more about environmental effects on bird variation, however, the significance of size and color differences in subspecies is no longer clear. Perceived differences between individuals may not reflect slowly evolved adaptations, but rather genetic flexibility. Creatures isolated in new habitats can change rapidly. Ornithologist Frank Gill cites studies of the red-winged blackbird, in which young hatched from eggs transferred to nests of foster parents in a different area take on morphological traits of the foster parents. Everglades redwings hatched near Tallahassee, Florida, grew shorter, thicker bills similar to their Tallahassee foster parents. Colorado redwings hatched in Minnesota developed longer wings and toes, again, resembling their foster parents in the new habitat. Coloration patterns of North American English sparrows are different than those of their European ancestors, a change that has occurred in less than 200 years. And even more recently, a Japanese scientist has demonstrated that feather color of domestic turkeys can be modified between molts by dietary differences. Morphological or color traits, then, may not always denote long-term adaptations but rather rapid adjustment to local environments or foods. Exactly how these realizations will influence the concept of subspeciation remains to be seen.

In 1999, working on her doctorate at Northern Arizona University (NAU) and using DNA analysis of tissues, Karen Mock substantiated genetically five of the existing wild turkey subspecific categories. This result was, in itself, significant above and beyond simple turkey classification. When many other wild species have been scrutinized by modern molecular genetics, earlier subspecific categories based on morphology have not always held up well. For example, the puma, the other species with which I am closely acquainted, was once split into as many as thirty-three subspecies scattered across the two Americas. Fourteen of these occurred on the North American continent. Recent genetics work on this species has reduced the total number of subspecies to six, and the number in North America to one.

Like McKusick, Mock found the Merriam's turkey to be more closely related to Eastern, Florida, and Rio Grande turkeys than to the Gould's turkey, and she supported Stangel in placing Gould's turkey genetically distant from the other subspecies. She was unable to acquire tissue from the South Mexican subspecies and hence left the status of that subspecies uncertain.

Mock's research was a culmination of eight years of planning and work that began as campfire sessions on Boulder Mountain near Escalante, Utah. Karen and her husband John helped me on a turkey habitat assessment project in that area in 1991. At the time, Karen was an instructor in biology at Yavapai College in Prescott, and the field project provided a welcome escape from laboratories and students. But Karen's field of specialization was microbiology and, as an instructor in a two-year junior college, she felt herself falling behind advances in her field. She yearned to complete a Ph.D. and perhaps go on to university teaching. Once she became aware of the need for a more complete assessment of turkey subspecies, her immediate future was determined.

She became acquainted with Dr. Paul Keim at NAU and discussed the feasibility of the project for a doctorate. Once it was accepted in concept, she went to work accumulating the necessary tissues from a wide geographical base. Finding material from relatively pure subspecific strains was in itself difficult because of the long history of transplanting and mixing of subspecies across the range of the turkey. Nonetheless, she was able to locate enough native populations to proceed.

Karen then searched for funding and found support from the National Wild Turkey Federation and the Arizona Game and Fish Department. At the time she started her work, the Turkey Federation and the Arizona Game and Fish Department were collaborating with Fort Huachuca to restore Gould's turkey populations to mountains in southern Arizona. As a part of her project, they wanted an assessment of the purity of the turkey population in the Huachuca Mountains, an area where Gould's turkeys had possibly been mixed with a purported, small remaining population of Merriam's from an earlier transplant. I will discuss her results regarding this population in another chapter.

Taking leave from her teaching job, Karen returned to school at NAU and developed the advanced skills in molecular genetics necessary for making the desired assessments. She now teaches at Utah State University and, among other projects, is cooperating with archaeologists from Washington State University to assess the origins of the turkeys found in Anasazi ruins, using tissue from the mummified turkeys at Mesa Verde National Park. And even this evaluation, remote as it may seem, has implications for modern turkey management, as we shall see in a later chapter.

4 Checking Things Out

One of the tools we used in wildlife management, more in the past than now for some reason, was the hunter check station. By stopping hunters at such stations, we could determine what proportion had killed game, and gather information on the sex, age, and condition of the animals being brought out. Check stations were used to make sure hunters were properly licensed, had attached tags correctly, and had adequately cared for their game. Check stations provided hunters with a known location to stop and ask for information on hunting regulations or wildlife distribution. Unfortunately, they also provided unsuccessful or chronically hostile hunters a place to vent their frustrations upon check station operators.

At one of our fall hunt check stations in the Moqui, Miles and I found ourselves being visited several times a day by an elderly gentleman riding an early version of trail bikes called a Tote-Goat. He was camped just down the road from the check station. He would zip into camp on his backcountry motor scooter, and frantically ask us a batch of questions about turkey hunting, turkey numbers, and, always, where he should try to find a turkey. We would suggest a place and he'd zip away with high hopes of killing a bird, sure that we had given him the best possible information. Within an hour or two, he'd be back, usually having seen nothing and wanting another suggestion. He always brought a treat of homemade cookies or banana bread, of which he seemed to have an unending supply. After a little more small talk and another deluge of questions, which we answered the best we could, off he'd go again, only to return after a short hunt, again unsuccessful. Finally, early in the afternoon on the last day of the opening weekend, he putted proudly into our station with a four-pound poult tied on the back of his scooter. He had scored at about the twentieth location that we had told him was the best possible place to kill a turkey. He was as excited as any hunter could be.

By this time, the weekend was well enough along that hunters were folding up camps and beginning to drift out of the woods. We often had two or three cars lined up as we checked dead birds, licenses, and tags. From past experience, we knew that this was the time of the season when, sooner or later, some angry hunter would unload on us about the inadequacy of our turkey management, the infringement of game laws on their rights, or sometimes both in the same breath. Such tirades were not always rational. As government employees, not knowing whom we might be dealing with, we learned to take our lumps, respond with polite "yes sirs" and "no sirs," check their bag carefully, explain what policies we could, and then get rid of them as rapidly as possible. The last thing we wanted to do was create a scene or push someone who was already angry into violent action.

As it turned out, our elderly friend was present when the inevitable irate carload arrived. In fact, he had been hanging around and telling hunting tales, almost as if he were killing time and avoiding going back to camp. He was pleasant and positive, even helpful on small things at the station, so we enjoyed having him around. The car in question held four hunters. I don't remember much about them, except that they had seen no turkeys, and proceeded to tell us about how we had destroyed the whole turkey population in northern Arizona with the new spring hunts, which hadn't yet happened on the Moqui. They also railed on our destruction of the deer population with our "doe hunts," which hadn't occurred for over five years. From all appearances, they had downed a few beers while breaking camp.

We tried to give polite responses, arguing gently with facts where we could and hoping the hunters would move on. They seemed more determined than most to have their say and were beginning to disrupt the functioning of the station. Cars were backing up behind theirs. I started to think I was going to have to ask them to leave and, because of their aggressive behavior, was dreading the possibility of a physical encounter of some kind. We were a long way from any kind of law enforcement backup.

Suddenly, our elderly guest arose from his camp stool, sternly straightened himself up to his full height, which was more imposing than I had noticed to this point, and stepped between us and the hunters. He then unleashed a tirade that made theirs sound puny. He told them how ashamed they should be to act the way they were; that we were fine, dedicated, underpaid professionals doing the best job we could and that they were bullies for taking advantage of the fact that as public servants we couldn't talk back. I tried to intervene, but he waved me back. He went on and on, giving the hunters no chance to reply. At first their anger seemed to surge, then they stood and listened with mouths open, seemingly puzzled and amazed. They began to shrink in size and one by one crept back to their car. He was still shouting through their car window as they drove away, trying to mumble apologies. He actually waved his fist at them as they went out of sight.

Miles and I stood watching, totally flabbergasted. As soon as the car disappeared, he turned to us with the grandest smile across this face. "You know," he said, "I spent thirty years working for the Nevada Game Department and took a load of that kind of shit. I've always wanted to do that." With that, he grabbed his turkey, leaped on his Tote-Goat, and putted down the road toward his camp. Miles, scratching his head and watching him disappear around a curve in the road said, "Who was that masked man?"

As you might understand, we had mixed feelings about check stations. Generally, the people we met were both pleasant and interesting. We made many new and lasting friends while checking hunters. We learned a lot about turkeys and heard dozens of hunting tales. Some were more memorable than others. One of my most unusual check stations occurred the year that we held the first spring hunt on the Moqui. Because we already had the "effects of hunting" study going there, the commission's creation of the spring hunt forced us to hold a spring as well as a fall check station. Only a few spring

permits had been allocated and the season lasted through two week-
ends, including the intervening weekdays. With such a hunt design,
we'd normally get a surge of hunters the opening weekend and very
few hunters in the woods thereafter. Nonetheless, we wanted a
complete check of hunters, so we decided to maintain the station
through the entire season. During the weekdays, we knew activity
would be minimal, so I decided to man the station by myself.

At the time, the Commission was uncertain about the best time
to hold a spring hunt. They had opened this season in early April; too
early, as we learned, to catch the gobbling peak that made for good
turkey calling. April weather in northern Arizona is always a bit unpredictable and usually cold and windy. But this April turned out to
be especially cold. In fact, snow set in before the season opened and,
before the week was over, we had eighteen inches of snow on the
ground. Even on opening day, virtually no hunters arrived. During
the week, I checked only one hunter. But I couldn't risk leaving the
station for fear of missing someone. By the end of the week, I was
sitting with my nose pressed against the window of the camp trailer
we used as lodging in the field, watching the rare car that passed
along the highway en route to the Grand Canyon, and wishing badly
for company of any kind.

The only respite I had from this lonely station was in the form of
another Arizona Game and Fish Department employee—a wildlife
manager named Don Moon, from Parker, Arizona. Don was on vaca-
tion and came to hunt spring turkeys. He had never hunted turkeys
in the spring and was determined to give it a try. He, with a friend
who was a deputy sheriff in the Parker area, camped down the road.
They had just finished ten days of working the Colorado River during
college spring break and were ready for some relaxation and recreation. The sheriff had confiscated fifty cases of beer from partying
juveniles, and the local judge had ordered them to destroy the beer.
He hadn't told them how. They had brought a portion of it along and
planned to "destroy" some of it in the evenings after they finished
their hunts. I didn't visit their camp to see if they really had such a
supply, but it made a good story. Considering the weather, it looked

like they would spend more time destroying beer than hunting turkeys. No one in his right mind would try to call a turkey in a blowing snowstorm.

But at that time, I didn't know Don very well. About the middle of the second morning, he dropped in the check station to check out a large gobbler. Snow had been falling all morning. I don't know if Don had ever called a turkey before, but he had dutifully taken his call to the woods, hunkered down with his back to a tree, and squawked away, not even sure he was making the right noise. The wind was such that you couldn't have heard an elephant bugle, much less a turkey gobble, but he stuck with his calling for an hour or more. He suddenly realized that before him was a tom turkey, unheard over the sound of the wind, strutting in a foot of snow. Needless to say he shot it.

Don spent the remainder of the week trying to repeat the performance for his partner, but to no avail. Don goes down in my books as second only to Fred Phillips, whom we will meet later in this book, as a devotee of turkey hunting.

5 Turkey Chess

By the early 1900s, wild turkeys had been extirpated over much of their range, both in the eastern United States and in the Southwest. The conservation ethic promoted by Teddy Roosevelt and Aldo Leopold brought on a surge of activities aimed at restoring game species during the first half of the twentieth century. In the case of wild turkeys, these activities were largely focused on restoring the bird to its historic range.

Such efforts ultimately brought about one of the greatest success stories in the history of wildlife conservation. Much of this success is due of late to efforts by the National Wild Turkey Federation, which has promoted turkey restoration to the point that at this time, huntable populations of wild turkey now exist throughout their historic range. Turkeys can be hunted in every state in the United States except Alaska. Populations also exist in Czechoslovakia, Germany, New Zealand, New Caledonia, and Flinders Island off of Australia. In addition to those in Arizona, Merriam's turkey populations now exist in California, Nevada, Utah, Wyoming, Montana, Nebraska, Idaho, Oregon, and Washington—all outside of the historic native range of the subspecies. Merriam's turkey genes may also be extant in the turkey populations in Minnesota, Alberta, and Czechoslovakia.

Early efforts at turkey restorations were not particularly successful. Initially, well-meaning private citizens, as well as some wildlife agencies, attempted raising domestic turkeys and returning them to the wild. Unfortunately, the necessary instincts for survival had long since been bred out of the domestic stock, and these restoration efforts succeeded only in creating unexpected farmyard flocks or well-

fed populations of predators. Turkey restoration efforts went hand in
hand with other programs aimed at importing exotic game birds, such
as the ring-necked pheasant, Hungarian partridge, and chukar partridge. For all of these species, use of pen-raised and relatively tame
birds for planting stock virtually guaranteed failure.

By the 1940s, biologists involved in wildlife restoration and introduction programs were converting to use of transplanted wild stock.
The history of these programs has been written before and is too
complex to be covered here. The technology that allowed restoration
of turkeys to succeed included improved trapping methods, improved
methods of holding and moving captured birds, and better understanding of turkey habitat needs.

Like the eastern subspecies, the Merriam's turkey had been extirpated over much of its range by about 1930, although relatively
large native populations existed in isolated areas, such as the Fort
Apache Indian Reservation and other sites along the Mogollon Rim.
By the 1940s, Arizona had a wildlife restoration program underway,
supported by Pittman-Robertson Funds generated through excise
taxes on sporting guns and ammunition. Restoration of turkeys was a
major effort within this program. It was carried out with considerable enthusiasm for several years. What it had in enthusiasm, however, it perhaps lacked in planning.

We have few records regarding many of these transplants and
even fewer regarding the thinking behind the decisions to plant birds
in particular areas. In some cases, the transplants were probably not
needed. For example, about 1990, my curiosity led me to seek out an
old timer who had worked in the Prescott National Forest during the
1940s and 1950s. During the 1950s, turkeys had been brought from
the Mogollon Rim and released near Juniper Mesa, northwest of
Prescott. I knew from early diaries that this area had held turkeys
prior to Anglo settlement, and I could find nothing to suggest that the
birds had ever been extirpated. I asked the elderly gent if he knew
whether any birds still lived on Juniper Mesa at the time the game
department brought in the new turkeys. "You know," he said, "I always wondered why they didn't put those turkeys up on top of the

mesa, where all the other ones were." Whether the transplant helped the existing population or not is unknown, but a good turkey population still exists on Juniper Mesa.

In addition to transplants made into areas where turkeys had historically occurred, turkeys were also planted in areas where they never before existed in Arizona, such as the North Kaibab and the Arizona Strip, north of the Grand Canyon. The North Kaibab population has done well; the populations on Mount Trumbull and Mount Dellenbaugh, less so. These latter areas have limited water availability and only small areas covered by ponderosa pine forest. It is unlikely that those mountains will ever hold large turkey numbers.

One of the more interesting aspects of these transplants north of the Grand Canyon involved technique. Because of the relatively remote locations of the target areas and their distance from where the birds were trapped, the transplant stock was flown to their new homes. Since landing strips were scarce, the birds were simply pitched out of the slow-flying airplane from a couple of thousand feet up and allowed to glide into their new habitats. They apparently found each other once on the ground, because the transplants did succeed. These Arizona transplants gained from at least one negative experience by eastern biologists, who first attempted air-dropping turkeys. These biologists, wanting to minimize trauma on the birds, had requested the pilot to fly low, so that the birds would not need to make long glides from abnormal heights. Their first drops were made from too low an elevation, and the birds failed to react quickly enough to their freedom. They didn't unfold their wings and fell to the earth like small bombs. None survived. Such are the travails of progress.

Much of Arizona's effort went toward restoring turkey populations to the southern mountain ranges in the state—the Chiricahuas, Huachucas, Santa Ritas, Catalinas, Rincons, and others—where the birds had been completely extirpated during the 1800s. These restoration efforts had mixed success. A good population of Merriam's turkey was established in the Chiricahua Mountains and exists there today. However, populations in the Huachucas, Santa Ritas, and Catalinas seemed to barely hold their own, in spite of repeated transplants to augment the earlier efforts. All of these restoration efforts used wild-trapped Merriam's stock from the Apache Reservation or points along the Mogollon Rim.

As wildlife biologists became increasingly aware of the various subspecies of wild turkey, a few knowledgeable individuals began to suggest that the southern mountain ranges of Arizona and New Mexico had not been within the historical range of the Merriam's subspecies. They developed increasingly convincing evidence that these southern habitats were more similar to and actually linked with the range of the Gould's turkey of the northern Sierra Madre.

Perhaps the first person to actively pursue this question was a district wildlife manager named Ron Anderson, who was stationed in Nogales, Arizona. He became interested in the history and origins of the turkeys in his area of responsibility, which included the Pajarito Mountains. Ron sought out specimens of turkeys from south of the border, and he tracked down the only existing specimen from the native population of turkeys in the Chiricahua Mountains. In the end, his efforts produced nothing conclusive, but he had brought the question to the forefront.

Amadeo Rea, an ethnobiologist living in San Diego, also became interested and compared the single Chiricahua specimen with turkeys from the Sierra Madre and from northern Arizona. He concluded that the original Chiricahua population had definitely been more closely related to the northern Mexican (Gould's) subspecies. Shortly after, New Mexico biologists discovered that a small population of turkeys living in the Peloncillo Mountains in extreme southwest New Mexico was of the Gould's race.

Because the straggling Merriam's turkey population in the Huachuca Mountains was gradually disappearing, and because no one was sure what the original native stock there had been, biologists at Fort Huachuca decided to try planting Gould's turkey stock from Mexico. Their early efforts in the 1980s were fraught with many frustrations, mostly brought about by difficulties in getting birds across the border and in satisfying quarantine legalities before the birds were released. Because of quarantine requirements, the first group of birds imported was held for several weeks in a large barnlike building at the Fort. By the time the quarantine period was over, a high percentage of the birds had died, some from simply battering themselves to death against the walls of the building.

But the biologists were persistent, and ultimately, with the cooperation of the Arizona Game and Fish Department, a population of turkeys was established. It has continued to grow and disperse, and flocks of wild turkeys now exist not only over much of the Huachuca Mountains, but also in the Canelo Hills and in the riparian woodlands of the San Pedro River. All of these birds are apparently a result of the Huachuca Mountain Gould's turkey transplants.

At the time these birds were imported, during the late 1980s, a few Merriam's turkeys apparently still existed on the mountain. Some concern was expressed that the established population was a mixture of the two races. As long as the birds did well, this was not a serious problem, except perhaps for purists in the hunter ranks who might someday want to add a Gould's turkey to their list of lifetime trophies. However, recent studies of DNA by Karen Mock, mentioned earlier, have demonstrated that the Fort Huachuca turkeys are pure Gould's turkey stock. Apparently none of the Merriam's turkeys had survived to breed, or if they did, the racial hybrids did not survive.

During the 1990s, the Arizona Game and Fish Department became interested in expanding the Gould's turkey transplant program and brought birds from Mexico to plant in the Galiuro Mountains. They have since supplemented these first transplants with birds trapped and moved from the now-successful Fort Huachuca population. The Galiuro transplant has not done well so far, and its fate is still uncertain. However, birds have been seen in pine forests on top of the mountain, several miles from the original transplant site, so hope for this population still exists.

Merriam's turkey restoration efforts still go on. Within the past decade, turkeys have once again been trapped on the Apache Reservation and moved to suitable but empty habitat on the Zuni Reservation. At this writing, these birds are doing well. At least some of this more recent success is due to our increasing understanding of the subtleties of turkey habitat requirements, including the realization the different subspecies are adapted to different habitats. If a restoration effort is to succeed, the transplant stock should come from a habitat that is similar to the area receiving the birds. Such understanding has come at least in part from habitat-related turkey research.

As is often the case, success has also attracted increased scrutiny, and turkey transplants have recently run into opposition in Colorado and California. In Colorado, biologists were concerned that competition from the larger bird, or possible introduction of disease, might reduce numbers of native ruffed or blue grouse. In California, biologists at Kings Canyon, Sequoia, Point Reyes, Lassen Volcanic, and Redwoods National Parks have opposed plans by the State Department of Fish and Game to plant turkeys in the mountains of northern California. Some state parks in California have also opposed the program. Once again, the National Wild Turkey Federation is the main force behind these transplants, but the organization is now being cast by some in the role of an ecological villain. Again, competition with native species is a concern, as well as contaminating national parks with a nonnative species.

The dialogue has become warm. A park service administrator has said, regarding the Merriam's turkey, "The problem with this particular species of turkey is it's something you really can't fix, once the genie is out of the bottle. Part of the reason the American people have set aside places such as Yosemite is because of their wild values and those values get compromised when you start putting other species in there."

At the other extreme, a Wild Turkey Federation director has countered, "This is a case of some zealots in the federal government trying to dictate to the state of California what they should and shouldn't do outside the parks. This is not turning feral pigs loose in the Garden of Eden."

At this writing, the issue is not resolved. It is not likely to be simple, already involving hunter interests, federal agencies, contradictory ecological concepts, and state's rights. Even our favorite American bird can become a point of contention.

6   If We Could Talk to the Animals

All during the time that we were trapping turkeys, I continued developing a new study plan. I wanted to shift the emphasis of the study to assessing the effects of logging—a land use that could drastically modify turkey habitat. The greatest difficulty in devising such a plan lay in establishing cooperation between the Arizona Game and Fish Department and the U.S. Forest Service, the agency that controlled most of the turkey habitat in Arizona. In the 1960s, everyone still operated under the assumption that good timber management was good wildlife management. The Forest Service managed the timber; we managed wildlife populations, which mainly meant we controlled hunters. Habitat was a vague notion that existed somewhere in between the two agencies' responsibilities.

Our approach to both research and management was basically reactive. Wildlife was considered by most people to be the least important resource on public lands, because it created no money, and commercial interests always held sway. As a result, virtually every study we designed was entitled "The Effects of *Blank* on *Blank*." You only had to fill in some human-caused factor operating on some species. "The Effects of Logging on Turkeys" was my stated concern. Other people looked at the effects of hunting on javelina, the effects of juniper eradication on deer, and so forth.

At that time, I don't believe wildlife biologists really thought much about changing the way logging was carried out. At best, we may have hoped to predict the effects and adjust hunt regulations in accordance with predicted turkey numbers. If anyone in the business world had suspected that our results might ultimately be used to challenge commercial uses of public lands, a few calls by logging executives to appropriate officials would probably have quickly ended the studies. Conversely, because we worked for a management agency, we never clearly acknowledged that we were really studying the basic habitat requirements of animals. We thought more in terms of discrete limiting factors within the environment. Habitat studies unattached to some land use practice would have been considered "pure" research—something universities did. We walked an interesting fine line, never clearly acknowledging to anyone, at times including ourselves, what we were actually trying to do.

In our defense, I might point out that the word *habitat* was only coming of vogue when we started the turkey work. The word did not even appear in Aldo Leopold's 1933 text *Game Management.* Its use had emerged slowly through the 1940s, 1950s, and 1960s as a rather vague notion in avian literature. We ultimately adopted the term into the jargon of the wildlife profession, but it was seldom mentioned elsewhere. Classical wildlife management spoke of food, water, and cover as requirements of a wildlife species. For most of us, habitat was synonymous with cover—the structural component of wildlife necessities. Only recently has the word habitat assumed the broader connotation of total wildlife needs, including food, water, cover, and, more important, the way in which these elements interact in the life history of a species. It now signifies the total necessities of life in the broadest and most dynamic sense. This viewpoint has changed the way we study turkeys.

Merriam's turkey research wasn't a new activity in the Southwest in 1965, and several studies had already looked at components of habitat. One of the earliest research projects funded by the Arizona Game and Fish Department was a 1939 assessment of Merriam's turkey populations. A then-young scientist named Lyndon Hargrave carried this out. After less than one year of field observations, Hargrave concluded that winter food shortage was the main limiting factor on Merriam turkeys. Unfortunately, Hargrave's tenure with the Arizona Game and Fish Department was short, reputedly because he felt that drumsticks from birds collected as specimens were a part of the fringe benefits of the job. The local game warden, probably already uneasy about new-fangled biology, apparently disagreed.

Turkey research ceased in Arizona during World War II. But work continued in New Mexico. U.S. Biological Survey biologist J. Stokely Ligon compiled his observations into a small book, *The Merriam's Turkey,* published in 1946 by the University of New Mexico Press. Ligon's book is still one of the best sources of information on historic population declines and original distribution of the Merriam's subspecies. Many of Ligon's ideas, formed through daily experience with unmarked turkey populations, hold up amazingly well under the scrutiny of modern radio-tracking studies.

Shortly after Ligon's work was published, a new generation of wildlife biologists, mostly World War II or Korean War veterans educated under the GI Bill, began to enter the wildlife field. These new specialists were steeped in the tradition of Aldo Leopold and were ready to apply scientific principles to solving wildlife management problems. To most of these young biologists, wildlife meant huntable species. A succession of biologists studied Merriam's turkeys between 1950 and 1965. Although many of their reports were never published in journals, each of these individuals contributed to our increased understanding of the bird. For Arizona, the names include Bob Reeves, Wendell Swank, and Robert Jantzen. Their studies dealt with food habits, predation effects, and winter range delineation.

In New Mexico, Levon Lee, Robert Spicer, and Duncan Mac-Donald contributed to our understanding of turkey behavior and habitat needs. In Colorado, Donald Hoffman made the first quantitative assessment of roosting sites and published a small handbook on turkey biology that was used for years by turkey biologists throughout the West. At the same time, workers outside of the historic range began to assess the factors affecting success or failure of transplanted populations in Nebraska, South Dakota, and Montana.

Through these projects, understanding of turkeys slowly increased. But two major problems plagued this work: lack of the continuity needed for well-planned and orderly development of information, and difficulties in directly observing this wary species. Also, while turkeys were interesting as a game species, they were no longer considered to be threatened. Increased game law enforcement had reduced the illegal kill that had devastated populations during the first decades of the twentieth century. And the success of restoration efforts in the Southwest created a complacency of sorts. If we lost turkeys in one place, we'd just catch a few somewhere else and put them back. As a result, turkeys received research attention only when issues surrounding more politically important species weren't pressing.

Through these years, logging in ponderosa pine forests was still done selectively, and the actual effects on the wildlife habitats were minimal. The ponderosa pine forests of Arizona's Mogollon Rim, running across nearly two-thirds of the state, were still fairly diverse: sapling thickets were interspersed with clumps of larger, older trees that were associated with a relatively open and grassy understory. Wildlife biologists were aware that the Forest Service was changing its approach to timber management, but we had no clear vision of what such changes would do to the landscape.[1] We had a fair number of turkeys to study, and we had begun to hope that useable radio-tracking equipment was on the way. An evaluation of effects of logging on turkeys seemed feasible. Time didn't seem to be a problem.

Also, by the late 1960s, two other biologists, Irv Boeker and Virgil Scott, had been assigned by the Fish and Wildlife Service to study turkeys on the Fort Apache Indian Reservation. As it turned out, their research was relatively short lived, but they added substantially to our knowledge of turkey food habits and provided important measurements of winter roost trees and roosting sites. But their work ended before good radio-tracking equipment became available; hence they were unable to evaluate seasonal movement patterns or habitat requirements. Boeker was actually a pilot-biologist with the Service and had a Cessna 180 assigned to the turkey project. Had he and Scott been able to work with radio-marked turkeys, they could have accelerated turkey research and added quickly to our knowledge of turkey seasonal movements and habitat use. But radio tracking was a tool yet to come.

7 Darwin? This is Merriam One, Come on Back

At the time Miles and I began turkey research, catching turkeys was merely the first step in gathering data, and we played a fine juggling act with our time. I worked on better study plans, we trapped turkeys when conditions allowed, we applied available study methods, and we tried to develop new technology that would give us better data. In the 1960s, the personal computer was unheard of, and radiotelemetry, allowing us to locate birds by fitting them with a miniature transmitter, was still a field biologist's fantasy. Turkeys were studied by direct observation when you were lucky enough to see them and by reading sign when you weren't. Data were analyzed on cumbersome desk calculators, plugging numbers into statistical equations from textbooks and tediously adding, subtracting, or multiplying one figure at a time. Square roots were estimated by slide rules or by extrapolating from tables in mathematical handbooks. Computers existed in big rooms somewhere on college campuses or in national defense installations. They required dozens of specialists to program them for even the simplest calculations.

For our tiny wildlife research budgets, use of computers was therefore out of the question. As a result, even without telemetry, we could rapidly gather more field data than we could ever hope to analyze. We had to choose our research objectives carefully. Also, because of the limitations of our field technique, any data we gathered could lead to erroneous conclusions. We tried hard to be aware of the weaknesses of our methods. By the late 1960s, a few people were experimenting with radiotelemetry, but no commercial equipment was yet available. So we applied the two time-tested methods mentioned earlier: colored tags placed on the birds, so that we could recognize them later, and roadside routes driven periodically to count and observe turkeys in a way that could be subjected to statistical analysis. Turkeys were actually more tolerant of vehicles than they were of biologists slipping through the woods on foot, so most of our observations were made while driving along two-track roads. We classified the birds' behavior and later measured habitat characteristics at each place we sighted undisturbed turkeys, and we made the same measurements on a larger sample of randomly located sites. These random sites provided a characterization of the range of available habitats against which we could compare the places where turkeys were actually seen—a way of comparing what habitats they had used with the array available to them.

We knew studies conducted in this manner were biased. For example, we knew we missed seeing turkeys in denser cover. Hence our sightings represented only use of the more open habitats. Also, our routes were run morning and evening, when turkeys were most likely to be out feeding. We could not detect the habitats being used for other forms of behavior, such as nesting and roosting. And we had no way to know how many birds ran away unseen at the sound of our oncoming vehicles.

Even the information acquired from the color-marked turkeys was limited. We rarely observed them after we marked them. Our few observations gave us scant insights into the distances that birds might move between seasons and the degree to which flocks intermixed. We made too few observations to detect any actual patterns. One exasperating aspect of color-marking birds involved sightings reported by people outside our project. Once the fact became generally known that color-marked birds roamed the woods, reports of sightings began to arrive. We rarely saw marked birds ourselves during our concerted field efforts, but seemingly everyone else did, if you could believe the reports. We learned early to ask polite questions regarding color and placement of markings, as well as where the marked birds were seen. More often than not, markers described were of colors we hadn't used and were attached to portions of the bird where placement would have been impossible. In some cases, reports came from areas so remote from any capture site that we had to view them skeptically. A few sightings came from habitats that made us wonder if the person had actually seen a turkey. Except for a few observers with known abilities, we discounted outside records. I hope that none of the people who had been kind enough to contact us ever read my annual reports.

During survey periods on the Moqui study area, we drove each route out and back morning and evening for five days, yielding twenty traverses of each fifteen-mile route. Most of these were along rough two-track roads, where you bounced incessantly over limestone ledges or basalt boulders. You fought reverie that made you forget to look for turkeys, and you fought the constant urge to drive as fast as conditions allowed, simply covering the required distance. At the end of one ten-day survey period, Miles commented, "I know that hell is an endless turkey survey route."

Personally, I never saw the routes as being quite that bad. While tedium certainly took its toll after several days, time spent slowly driving back roads and recording the wildlife was pleasant duty. It also produced a lot of data, at least for that time. Habitat measurement was less exciting. At each site, we recorded crown cover, hiding cover, ground cover, and a host of other habitat-related information. We hoped to relate our findings to changes that logging might make in the forest configuration. This was the bread and butter phase of the study—the work that kept data coming in, while we tried to improve our methods.

About 1970, radio tracking slowly began to become a reality. This technique, once available, would open the door to more detailed studies of habitat selection, overcoming the biases inherent in the direct observations that we were using on the routes. But successful application of radio tracking did not happen overnight. Many early efforts involved home-brewed transmitters developed by biologists with some electronics background (HAM radio operators, etc.) or biologists aided by radio experts interested in wildlife. Many people expended tremendous energy, but wildlife placed unexpected demands on electronic equipment, and the early radio-tracking efforts yielded little biological information.

In Arizona, we badly needed radio-tracking equipment for our studies on turkeys and javelina. We tried several strategies to develop equipment. I attended technician-level courses in radio technology at Northern Arizona University (NAU) and studied electronics with the help of local Bell Telephone technicians. I tried to build my own equipment, using citizen's band (CB), the only legal frequencies available at the time. None of my home-brewed equipment worked. My single transmitter, built after months of study, could barely be received across my small office on the NAU campus. At that time, use of CB radios was a growing fad among truckers and tourists on the highways. Nearly everyone had radios in their vehicles, and many had bases at home. They chattered incessantly. The weak signal of my experimental unit was buried under volumes of static produced by "breaker, breaker, come on back, good buddy."

An interested HAM operator in Tempe built improved equipment for us, but it was still on CB. His receivers were more sensitive and more portable than the equipment we had tested in our initial experiments. But his transmitters were low in power, his antennas inefficient, and the incessant banter over the airwaves continued to make the equipment unusable. In addition to this, his transmitters came in modules, and we had to solder battery, antenna, and transmitter together when we placed them on the birds at the trap site. Simply finding portable electronic tools to do such a job was difficult. Cordless electric soldering irons were unheard of, and connecting fine wires on flailing birds using soldering irons heated over a camp fire or a single-burner camp stove became a comedy worth filming. I'm glad that those of us involved in the work were the only witnesses. It's a miracle we didn't set the woods on fire.

Once the radios were installed, busy beaks, the day-to-day movement of birds through brush, and flailing wings destroyed these fragile transmitters as fast as we installed them. After months of searching, I finally received a signal from a turkey wearing one of these primitive units. I saw the bird in a flock of turkeys that crossed the road in front of my pickup, and I recognized its colored marker. I jumped out of my pickup and turned on the receiver just in time to hear two faint beeps before the bird disappeared into the forest. Once the turkey was out of sight, the signal died.

At this time, Jerry Day, working on javelina in southern Arizona, found a small electronics company in Tucson that changed the direction of our efforts. This company, called Sensory Systems Laboratory, built equipment on the two-meter band. No radio frequencies had yet been allocated to wildlife research, and use of UHF undoubtedly violated Federal Communications Commission (FCC) regulations. Our units were so low in power, however, that we hoped their faint beeps would go unheard by authorities. Using the airwaves illegally was probably not all that bold, but for those of us working in a regulatory agency, violating another agency's rules was a step we did not make without some anxiety. If higher-ups in the game department were aware of our transgressions, they did not acknowledge it. We weren't given to unnecessary confession.

The use of higher frequencies solved two major problems we faced in using CB. We no longer dealt with badly cluttered airwaves, and we could use more efficient antennas. Radio frequency or wavelength, normally measured in meters, determines antenna length. Citizen's band at that time was limited to the thirty-meter range. An efficient antenna for this wavelength was about half that or about fifteen meters in length. Homes of CB users could be spotted by antenna installations on their roofs that dwarfed their TV antennas. With coils and capacitors, antennas could be shortened for use on vehicles, but whip antennas eight to ten feet long attached to fenders were still a common sight. Each shortening of the antenna reduced its efficiency both in transmitting and receiving. With relatively powerful transmitters in vehicles powered by strong auto batteries, this was not a problem, but these inefficient antennas could not detect our puny signals at distances beyond a few hundred yards. And using efficient antennas on the transmitters was impossible. Allowing a turkey to drag a fifteen-meter antenna around the woods was obviously out of the question, although it's a wonder we didn't try it. Antennas on the two-meter band could be reduced to about fifteen inches in length and still be fairly efficient.

This new equipment worked well on the shop bench, but problems arose in the field. Electronic components available at that time were fairly small, but battery technology lagged far behind. To get a combination of signal strength and battery life to make the unit worth installing, we would have had to use batteries too heavy for our birds. Instead, we were forced to use smaller batteries that ran down in only a few weeks.

In addition to battery problems, we were still struggling with suitable methods of packaging the units. The transmitters we received from Sensory Systems were adequately encased in a durable plastic, but the battery pack was separate. Packaging the unit on the bird was up to us. This translated to wrapping everything with gobs of electrician's tape. We still had to solder battery leads to the transmitter on flailing birds at the capture site.

Once again, the birds destroyed most of the units as quickly as they were installed. The stainless steel antennas, soldered at one small tab, dropped off in the woods; wires connecting battery and transmitters broke; and transmitters that continued to function didn't necessarily produce useable radio waves in the wild. For normal communication uses, antennas for both transmitters and receivers are placed at optimum, usually elevated and highly exposed, locations (car tops, housetops, mountaintops). Every effort is made to keep them away from any surrounding bodies that might absorb signals or create unwanted signal bounce—a real problem if you are concerned about signal directionality. Our work required an antenna attached closely to the body of the turkey, which apparently absorbed and modified the wavelength being emitted. And, of course, the wild birds did not cooperatively check in from mountaintops, so that we could determine their position. The habitats they selected, dense forest and canyons, had all of the attributes that created signal distortion, loss, and bounce, reducing the accuracy of any locations we were able to make. Even with this new equipment, we spent many days in the woods listening for beeps that never came, or searching in the wrong places for those that did.

Insofar as our radio-tracking work was concerned (and that of many other biologists over the world, as it has turned out) the final breakthrough came in the person of an electronics wizard named David Beaty. Dave wandered into the Arizona Game and Fish Phoenix office sometime around 1966 or 1967. He was an Arizona native, raised at the Grand Canyon. He liked to hunt and fish. When he first contacted our department, he was working for Motorola, attending college to complete his degree in electronics, playing regularly in a local band, taking an active role in his church, and supporting a growing family. There didn't seem to be much remaining time to volunteer.

Nonetheless, Dave approached Steve Gallizioli, then chief of the research division for the department, and offered his help. He took one of our receivers home to analyze. Seemingly overnight, Dave was back in the Phoenix office with our receiver, now modified. "I think that will work better," he said. It did.

Dave then attacked the problem of improving our transmitters, focusing first on batteries and antennas. Over the next year, Jerry Day and I traveled from Tucson and Flagstaff, respectively, to spend hours climbing the buttes east of Mesa, Arizona, where Dave lived, to test range and directionality of new transmitters. For Jerry and me, the greatest improvement in the process was Dave himself. He acknowledged early that things were different in the woods than they were on the shop bench. Dave did his best to give us tools that required minimal knowledge of electronics on our part. He also improved packaging and installation, giving us time to concentrate on catching animals, attaching radios, and studying wildlife.

Although Dave's equipment was instantly better than anything we had tried, he continued to improve it. Amidst his busy schedule, he found time to build equipment for use on turkeys, javelina, and deer. He soon received requests for collars to fit desert bighorn sheep and mountain lions. Both lions and bighorn created special packaging problems. A lion could tear the transmitters to shreds; bighorn rams shattered transmitter crystals during their head-butting sprees. Dave tackled each new challenge with enthusiasm and creativity, developing better material to protect the collars and ways of protecting crystals.

Word soon spread that Arizona had telemetry equipment that

worked, and biologists in other states began to call. Within months, Dave had a cottage industry. Demand quickly overwhelmed this approach. A home shop and part-time help no longer sufficed. Dave quit his job, hired permanent employees, and leased a suite in downtown Mesa. Demand again overwhelmed this small establishment, and the company moved into a modern industrial building. Telonics, Inc. now employs some eighty people. Its radio-tracking equipment has been used on everything from bats to whales, and the company now provides centralized facilities for monitoring animals by satellite.

8 Wings and Prayers

At the time I'm writing this chapter, radio tracking of wild animals has become commonplace. We hardly consider an animal studied unless it has worn a transmitter for a high percentage of its life. In designing research, we now assume that we will be able to monitor the daily routine of a representative sample of individuals within a population. But we did not reach this point quickly. Even after suitable radio-tracking equipment became available, due largely to the efforts of entrepreneurs like Dave Beaty, we still had much to learn in applying it to research.

As in all wildlife research, our learning period was interrupted by the vagaries of weather and the uncertainties of equipment, coupled with our own naiveté on many matters. Even before Dave Beaty came into our lives, we had hung various versions of radio transmitters on turkeys. Although the equipment from the Tucson Sensory Systems Lab was fragile, it transmitted adequate signals to monitor the birds. During the spring of 1967, Miles and I assembled three of those units on mature gobblers. The area chosen, the Beaver Creek Experimental Watersheds lying about thirty miles south of Flagstaff, enclosed a wide variety of habitat modifications related to watershed research. Within the range of the turkeys we trapped was everything from clearcuts to strip cuts to thinnings to unlogged controls. It seemed a good place to observe turkey responses to human manipulation of forests.

We trapped the birds on winter range, at the lower edge of the ponderosa pine belt. When we returned with receivers, to listen for beeps, we heard nothing. After several days of cruising rough roads, we decided that air support was needed to get us above the intervening terrain that screened the signal. We needed line-of-site contact with every nook and cranny in the woods. This was virtually impossible from the ground. At that time, using an airplane was not a small decision. Wildlife research wasn't a high priority activity within the department. Acquiring a four-wheel drive vehicle for fieldwork required special dispensation from the director's office. We had to need it badly and justify it thoroughly. Even buying snow tires for our two-wheel drive pickups required special written justification. We therefore knew that a request for use of the department Cessna to search for two or three turkeys was going to initiate major administrative trauma. We weren't sure that the pilot, accustomed as he was to flying dignitaries around the state, would lower himself to haul field biologists and search for *wildlife*. We also had no idea if the tracking antenna would work inside the plane.

As it turned out, we were right about the trauma created within the bureaucracy, but we were wrong about the pilot. Acquiring approval to fly required patience, paperwork, and a circumspect phone call or two. A couple of weeks passed before such a heavy decision could be made, during which time we continued our unsuccessful ground search for the radio-marked birds. On the morning the plane was to arrive, we made final tests of the receiver, using a spare transmitter. It wasn't working. The company that had built it was in Tucson, 250 miles away. In a panic, we called the radio technician at the state highway department shop in town to see if he could help. He said he'd try. He was still working on our receiver when the airplane arrived, and we went hat in hands to the airport, fully expecting the pilot to fly away in a huff. Instead, we only had to bear a moderate amount of friendly needling while we drove him to the nearest coffee shop. An hour later, the radioman had found a small fuse blown by a power surge, scrounged a replacement from a defunct highway department radio, and sent us on our way. I doubt that he has any idea how deeply grateful we were. Within thirty minutes after takeoff, we had located one of the turkeys. The other two radios had apparently failed. Nonetheless, at least within our own department, this event demonstrated the need to combine aircraft with radio transmitters if wildlife telemetry was to succeed. Few studies are designed today without the assumption that animals will need to be regularly relocated from the air.[1]

Receiver antennas were also a problem. None of the small, highly directional antennas now used in radio tracking were available to us at the time we started. The best we could find were multi-element yagis (similar to old VHF rooftop TV antennas) that were about three feet long and wide. These were designed for permanent installation on rigid mounts, and none of the available cable connectors were made to withstand the rigors of field transport. We quickly assembled a pack of field tools and became fairly innovative at repairing antenna cable.

Our original plan for radio tracking birds had been to monitor them from mountaintops with directional equipment, take fixes from two or more locations, and plot their movements in and around the watersheds by way of triangulation. As support for this, I had designed and built two twelve-foot yagi antennas mounted on tripods with compass discs. These could be quickly assembled and oriented. A student in forestry from Northern Arizona University spent weeks on a special studies project testing the directional accuracy of these antennas. They didn't work particularly well, but they were the best we had. We were laboriously entering the world of high tech.

Our single flight showed that our radio-marked bird had moved to its summer range, and was therefore no longer anywhere in the vicinity of the experimental watersheds. We spent the summer monitoring its movements and plotting its roost sites in an unlogged area around a meadow, five miles from anything we had planned to study. Because we hadn't anticipated working outside of the treated areas, we really weren't sure, other than daily movements, what kind of data to record.

We continued to locate this bird through the fall, all the while gearing up to trap more during the coming winter. But nature intervened. In mid-December, 1967, a weeklong storm dropped eight feet of snow in Flagstaff. Even the turkey winter range near the experimental watersheds was covered with a four- to five-foot layer. We had no idea where our turkey had gone, or whether it was still alive.

Emergency funds became available due to the snowstorm, and

we acquired a snowmobile—something we had never had reason to use in Arizona. Weeks passed before a few roads into the general area of the watersheds were cleared. Finally, one day I was able to take the snowmobile to the top of Apache Maid Mountain, overlooking the study area and, to my amazement, actually received a faint beep from somewhere to the northwest. Getting to the top of the mountain and back to camp before dark was a full day's work, so the next day, Miles and I were out on the snow machine early, intending to reach a high point nearer to the source of the signal. We weren't certain if the transmitter was still on a turkey or if the turkey was still alive, although variations in the signal received the day before had suggested that the transmitter was moving.

At the time, snowmobiles weren't a common item in Arizona. What we didn't know was that they worked best on packed trails or heavily crusted snow. We straddled the machine and headed out cross-country, with me steering and Miles trying to hang on behind while also grasping the antenna and receiver. Within minutes after leaving the plowed road, we were wallowing in four-foot deep snow on a creature that bogged down more than it moved. When it did move, it ran uncontrollably under low-hanging trees or skidded up against stumps. We spent more time trying to lift the four-hundred-pound monster out of holes than we did moving forward. Finally, in a more open stand of high-limbed trees, I was finally sailing along fairly well and actually headed in the right direction when I felt a lurch and heard a sound from behind that sounded something like "GLUCK!"

By the time I stopped the machine and started wallowing back through the thigh-deep snow, Miles was gathering himself out of the snow and trying to undo the half-hitched antenna cable from around his neck. The antenna, separated from the cable, was hanging on tree branch behind him. Fortunately, Miles' neck had been stronger than the antenna connector. The damage to the cable was irreparable in the woods, so we wallowed back to our field camp in an old-style mobile home and spent the rest of the day trying to re-solder the cable connection with our primitive equipment. We couldn't make it work. Finally, at dusk, we gave up and settled in for the night. By this time I had developed a severe headache and a good case of indigestion. The brandy we had brought for evening relaxation didn't look good. I rummaged through the drawers of the trailer and found a bottle of Alka-Seltzer that someone had left behind. Drawing a glass of water, I leaned back on the tattered couch to sooth my agonies. I dropped the wafer into the glass, and it just sunk to the bottom and sat there. It didn't fizzle. It didn't even slowly dissolve. Miles says I became a little hysterical at this point. He couldn't tell whether I was laughing or crying.

The next day, we made a quick trip to town to make repairs, and then stubbornly set out again on the snowmobile. After another two hours of wallowing, we covered about half a mile. Miles finally lost his patience with the machine and with me. "You know," he said. "This job was hard enough before we started carrying this four-hundred-pound son-of-a-bitch around with us." I agreed. We went home. I periodically returned to monitor the turkey from the one accessible mountaintop for the remainder of the winter. It stayed a long ways away from the watersheds.

9 The Best Laid Plans of Men and Turkeys

I hoped to shift our studies from the Moqui to the Beaver Creek watersheds, because of vegetation modification studies already being carried out there by the U.S. Forest Service. Areas averaging about two hundred acres had been cleared, strip cut, or thinned to varying levels of tree density to evaluate the effects of such modifications on water run-off. Studies of the effects of these vegetative treatments on deer and elk were already underway, so Beaver Creek seemed a natural choice as a place to document wild turkey responses to changing vegetation and logging practices.

The area, in fact, had a history of turkey research. Bob Reeves and Wendell Swank had used it as a study site in the 1950s for food habits and winter range assessments, so we even had some background information. Our approach to the project was simple. We would radio tag a sample of turkeys within the boundaries of the watershed treatment areas, then locate them frequently enough to determine the percentage of their time spent in the various watersheds.[1] Because additional watershed treatments were planned, we hoped to gather at least some before-and-after-treatment data.

This was not a perfect design. It was opportunistic. The various timber thinnings and clearings were not intended for evaluation of the kind of changes that logging would later bring about. But there was little chance of developing a habitat manipulation project on forestlands for the single purpose of assessing turkey habitat needs. We took our data where we could get it. At this time, we really had no particular hypothesis to test. Our work was largely descriptive.

This lack of clear direction ultimately created difficulty in getting the project funded. Our money was from Pittman-Robertson funds administered by the U.S. Fish and Wildlife Service. Pittman-Robertson funds came from excise taxes on sporting guns and ammunition. One federal coordinator stationed in Albuquerque administered our projects in Arizona. People in this job changed rapidly, so we rarely knew whom we would need to satisfy with a given proposal. Some would accept anything recommended by our department; others scrutinized each study as if the funds were coming from their own pockets. At the time I was developing the new turkey habitat research proposal, our coordinator from Albuquerque was one with more miserly inclinations.

On his annual inspection tour, the Pittman-Robertson man targeted the turkey study for special review. After a day in Phoenix, gaining an overview of the department's total research effort, he traveled to Flagstaff and devoted a full day to a sentence-by-sentence inquisition of my proposal. In retrospect, I know I should have appreciated the extra attention. The man was simply doing his job. As a young biologist, I felt threatened.

Nonetheless, after several hours of questions, the coordinator gave the project his approval. I can't say he was excited about it, but he seemed to feel that it was worthwhile. The next day, I incorporated his recommendations into my study plan and left my office feeling that, after three years of stumbling around on the obsolete "effects of hunting" project, we were at last moving toward something of lasting value.

But the phone was ringing when I walked through the door at home. It was my Phoenix-based supervisor calling to tell me that our department had decided to end the turkey project. The politics of mountain lions in the state had created a new crisis, and biologists were being reassigned. Turkeys had bottom priority.

I won't go into the maneuverings and manipulations that followed this decision, but I must admit that I had begun to question the wisdom of people who chose to rise in our agency. Nonetheless, with the support of my immediate supervisor, I salvaged a part of the turkey project—the one on the Moqui that I had previously been trying to eliminate. We had gathered three years of roadside survey data from that hunting effects study area, and also had limited information on movements of color-tagged birds. By sheer coincidence, the Forest Service was planning to log eight thousand acres in the heart of the best summer and fall turkey habitat in that study area. If we could continue our roadside surveys for at least two years after the heavy logging program, we could see what the short-term response of turkeys to such a drastic timber harvest might be. The project would be a minimal effort with many design flaws. But it was better than a total loss of the three years of work already spent. Before the month was over, I was writing lion research plans, and we were hiring a graduate student to wrap up the existing turkey project.

In keeping with our fears regarding logging effects on turkeys, during the 1970s, and especially the 1980s, the Forest Service gradually shifted to even-aged management of ponderosa pine, wherein they cut the older trees and left younger ones. The purpose was to create a forest of uniform size and shape that could be logged economically by cutting all the trees in an area at one time. In most areas, the immediate change in the forest landscape wasn't drastic enough at any given time to cause excitement. It wasn't until the second or third cutting over a ten- to fifteen-year period had occurred that wildlife biologists began to worry seriously about the effects of such timber management on turkeys and other species. By then, much of the forest was already composed only of trees measuring six to twelve inches in diameter, which were sparsely and evenly spaced over the landscape. No one was monitoring the effects of these changes on turkeys. Had not one concerned individual spoken out, every tree big enough to provide roosts would probably have been removed from Arizona forests. That individual was an Arizona Game and Fish Department wildlife manager named Fred Phillips.

During the time that Miles and I had been trying to catch turkeys, Fred had become intrigued with the turkeys in his district, which lay south of Williams, Arizona. Research was not part of Fred's job. His responsibilities included game surveys, fisheries surveys, public relations, and all game law enforcement for an area encompassing some one thousand square miles. He had no obligation to take on extra work, nor, it would seem, did he have the time. Also, as in most bureaucracies, extraordinary effort was often viewed askance by less ambitious peers and carried the risk of increased scrutiny by administrators, who wondered if the regular duties of the job were suffering.

Nonetheless, when our turkey work ended, Fred took up our tools and went to the woods. Over the next three years, he became a master turkey trapper, refining methods far beyond the level that we had reached in our meager efforts. Fred liked to trap turkeys, a job that neither Miles nor I relished. Miles had left Montana to ease his arthritis, and sitting immobile in near-zero weather had not been his Arizona dream. For me, catching turkeys was merely a means to an end. I wanted marked birds to study, and I wanted them marked with minimum effort. Thus trapping was a necessary evil to be endured until we could get on with the real work.

Fred was not encumbered by any of these prejudices. He enjoyed watching turkeys under any circumstances. He became obsessed with the turkey trapping and soon moved away from the projectile nets altogether. Because he was working alone, he needed a method that did not result in a dozen or more birds flailing and defoliating under a net.

As mentioned earlier, I had built several portable wooden traps with self-activated drop gates, the modern version of the "pole traps" used by Indians and early settlers. During a year of experimenting with these traps, I had managed to catch only one turkey hen and one Brittany spaniel (my own). With all of its problems, the projectile net had produced more birds for us.

Fred absconded with the panel traps. He developed their use into a fine art. He didn't mind sitting in blinds, and he could contentedly watch turkeys for hours, whether they entered his trap or not. Being unencumbered by formalized research plans, he could simply take knowledge about turkeys in whatever form it arrived. He had no rigid mental program that said "mark first, study later." He baited turkeys into the panel trap sites and studied their responses to traps and to each other. As a result, he began to capture turkeys in large numbers.

Fred discovered early that baiting technique was critical in trapping. Like most gallinaceous birds, turkeys develop a peck order in their flocks. A dominant bird will take over a small pile of oats and keep all other birds away. With the projectile nets, we were baiting birds into large enough areas that intra-flock behavior had not greatly influenced our results. (Although even here, Fred has since shown us that proper dispersion of bait would have increased the catch.) With the panel nets, proper placement of bait in and around the trap determined the rate at which birds entered the gate and how many birds would actually go in. Bait near the entrance would be taken over by a dominant bird, blocking any other from entering. Small piles scattered toward the rear of the trap gave several birds places to feed.

Our use of the panel traps had been motivated by a degree of laziness. We simply wanted to visit them midday and mark turkeys. The whole idea was to use drop gates that the birds tripped by hitting a string across the rear of the trap. Fred enjoyed watching the birds, and he modified the traps so that he could drop the gate from his blind. As a result, he could wait for the maximum number of birds before pulling the string. He could then crawl in the trap with the birds, bag them, retreat to a comfortable place, and mark them more or less at his leisure. Modern turkey trapping, whether with a net or panel, has incorporated many of the techniques that Fred and a few others like him quietly developed, usually without the fanfare of journal publications or other excursions of the ego. In terms of biological knowledge, Fred's larger sample of marked turkeys revealed larger seasonal movements than any of us had imagined. Some of his birds showed up as far as forty miles from the trap site.

For all of his effort, Fred's work was nonetheless opportunistic and he based many of his ideas on impressions developed from observations made during routine patrol of his district. Information such as size of daily home range and detailed habitat selection behavior could not be documented through such informal study. We still needed better information about daily and seasonal turkey habitat requirements, a point Fred made amply clear in his written report.

Fred was the first biologist in Arizona to suggest that logging on

forestlands had already gone awry and to request that wildlife biologists have some influence on land management decisions. A letter
Fred submitted to the Kaibab National Forest in the mid-1970s, de-
crying loss of turkey roosts as a result of logging sent reverberations
through the southwestern region of the Forest Service. Foresters,
believing that good timber management was good wildlife management, had been selling timber at unprecedented rates. Their goal was
to create an orderly, even-aged forest that could be logged over large
areas at minimum cost to industry. Such management made them
heroes to the logging industry, but it made them less than popular
with people concerned with wildlife.

The Kaibab National Forest responded to Fred's criticisms with
minimum efforts to save a few turkey roosts, usually in stands of trees
that weren't particularly suitable for logging. Fred asked for more,
and the Forest grudgingly saved roost sites that he, personally, had
marked. I'm sure the timber people assumed the whole thing would
go away. But Fred had created a crack in the armor of unrestrained
commercialism, and other biologists also began to challenge the system. Before long, directives were issued for the entire southwestern
region of the Forest Service that designated the number of roost sites
to be saved per square mile for each timber sale. The process for
selecting roosts remained somewhat mechanical, but at least one
species of wildlife was finally being considered in timber management plans.

10 Of Turkeys and Hunters

Some fifteen years passed before I was again involved with turkeys. During this time, policies regarding turkey hunting continued to change, as did the philosophies and attitudes of hunters. I've not discussed hunting much to this point, so perhaps this is a good time to do so. The subject is covered in dozens of books and outdoor magazine articles, so I won't go into great detail.

The best turkey hunting story I've ever heard was from Fred Phillips. It's worth telling here, because it gives a view of spring hunting, and it also helps to further characterize Fred, his interest in turkeys, and his devotion to turkey hunting.

In addition to perfecting the art of turkey trapping, Fred loved to call turkeys. He would call turkeys just to watch them; he would call turkeys during season to hunt them; he would travel to other states to call turkeys; he would call turkeys for friends who wanted to hunt. He liked to call turkeys.

As his skills advanced, Fred became more discriminating in the way he hunted turkeys. He became so skilled that he could pick an appropriate stand for calling, conceal himself, and then predict the spot to which he would bring the bird before he would shoot it. He would keep calling until he brought the bird to that spot.

Turkey calling is mainly a spring activity. You call the male bird by imitating the enticing call of a receptive female. In Merriam's turkey country, gobblers can be heard gobbling, especially during morning hours, throughout the spring, with peak gobbling activity from late April through May. Normally, the hens hearing the call come to the male. But an ardent male also drifts toward the answering hen and, if she doesn't rapidly close the gap between them, may search her out. On this, spring turkey hunters must depend. In spring turkey hunting, you shoot only gobblers, leaving the hens to nest and produce young.

True turkey hunting aficionados almost always hunt in the spring. Fred is an aficionado. He proved this on the day our story occurred. He was hunting in the White Mountains of Arizona one morning and, with his usual skill, had begun to work a gobbling male to his blind. The bird was close, actually in sight, but had not quite reached the point at which Fred had decided to take his shot. Fred had already shouldered his shotgun and was talking to the bird with a small calling device in his mouth. Suddenly, the bird went into a strange behavior pattern, circling and expressing alarm. Fred was certain that he had said nothing with the call that alerted the bird. His spiel had been the standard plaintive yelp of the interested hen. Yet the gobbler was obviously upset, ceasing to strut and walking in an indecisive circle. Fred was puzzled, but skillfully kept the bird from departing by increasing the sensuality of his yelps.

Then Fred, growing a bit weary from holding the shotgun to his shoulder, saw a slight movement out of the corner of his eye. Any movement of his head would have spooked the turkey, so Fred shifted his eyes as far toward the movement as he could while holding his body still. He was amazed to discover a puma that, like the gobbler, had been attracted to Fred's call. Unlike the gobbler, the puma had a meal, rather than a romp in the forest, in mind. It was only about ten yards away.

A normal hunter would have at this point done one of two things: jump up and scream or shoot the puma. Fred did neither. He calmly continued to talk to the gobbler in plaintive but reassuring terms, and very slowly shifted his shotgun to point at the cat. Quietly under his breath he said, "shoo, shoo, get out of here," and snapped his fingers at the puma. Amazingly, his strategy worked. The big cat realized that Fred was not a turkey, ceased its stalk, and sat on its haunches with a puzzled look on its face. When this happened, Fred turned his attention back to the bird, talked it into place, and shot it. When he looked back for the puma, it had disappeared.

Unlike Fred, I'm not a turkey caller. I've called in a dumb bird or two, but it's not something that I'm inclined to pursue to perfection. Nor am I much of a turkey hunter. I've hunted turkeys. I've shot a few, but not during spring hunts. But managing turkeys for hunters has largely driven the research I discuss in this book.

As I mentioned earlier, when I first started working on turkeys in 1965, spring hunting was not allowed. Spring hunting of gobblers was more a tradition of eastern hunters. In the West, we hunted birds in the fall, which is more like hunting any other upland game bird. During fall, the turkey population is near its annual peak, and a high percentage of the birds are young of the year. Any turkey can be taken, including mature hens, gobblers, or half-grown poults. Most fall turkey hunters still-hunt, moving quietly through the woods, then sitting for a while, then moving again. Or they may sit near a water hole, hoping to ambush birds coming to drink. Calling does not work as well in the fall as during the spring breeding season. If one happens to break up a flock of turkeys in the fall, calling the dispersed birds is a good way to get a turkey. Otherwise, calling is kind of a crapshoot. Sometimes it works, sometimes not. Quite often, undisturbed turkeys moving in a flock will not answer a call but may quietly approach the caller. Thus, unlike spring hunting, where the process involves talking to a gobbling male as he approaches, fall callers may not know if they are calling a bird or not. Fall calling requires a lot of patience. Few hunters do it.

While growing up in Arizona, I had hunted turkeys only once or twice and had been unsuccessful. After I took over the turkey study, the editor of the game department's magazine *Wildlife Views* asked me to write an article about our project. He also asked that I put a little into it about turkey hunting to attract the hunters' interest. By this time, I had trapped a few turkeys and was beginning to learn a little about their day-to-day habits. I still hadn't shot one myself and, in fact, was probably less interested in hunting than when I began the project. Trapping and handling live creatures always dampened my hunting inclinations. The living animal, because of what it could teach, became much more valuable than a trophy in hand.

Nonetheless, in writing the article for the magazine, I was obligated to add a short "how to" section on turkey hunting, most of which I derived from literature or from turkey hunters with whom I was acquainted. I wrote at length about the objectives of the study, the tools we were using, and what we were learning. At the end, I dutifully added a few pages on still-hunting of turkeys in the fall, emphasizing the use of stands near water sources that turkeys were known to frequent. In our dry western habitats, water limits turkey movements much more than in wetter eastern forests.

When the article was published, virtually all the information I had written about the study had been removed, and only the portion on hunting methods was published. The article touted me as an expert on the subject. The damage was done, so I didn't complain, but I carefully avoided talking about turkey hunting to anyone who broached the subject over the next few months. If I was an expert, I was determined to be a silent expert. I wanted no one to discover my true level of ignorance on the matter.

Finally, the fall hunt again arrived, and research assistant Norm Woolsey and I were running a hunter check station on the Moqui. I felt strongly that I had to hunt a turkey successfully, if for nothing more than to test the methodology I had recommended in the article. So, on the second morning of the season, I arose early and left Norm to open the check station. I went to a small stock tank that seemed to be relatively unknown by hunters. Tracks around it told me a small flock of mature gobblers was watering there. Before daylight, I was sitting overlooking the tank, using some low-hanging branches of an alligator juniper as a natural blind. About an hour after sunup, three large gobblers quietly slipped to the edge of the tank and began to drink. I selected one that was slightly apart from the other two, thereby eliminating the danger of my shotgun pattern encompassing more than one bird. I held on the gobbler's head and squeezed the trigger. He dropped and the other two disappeared into the forest. It had all been too easy. I returned to the check station as a successful hunter, but I felt no more like an expert than when I had departed. Since that time, I have killed several other turkeys, all during fall hunts.

Like many wildlife biologists trained in Leopoldian wildlife management, I have always assumed that regulated fall hunting could not hurt a turkey population. This belief was based on the concept of compensatory mortality, which says that over the stressful period of winter, a certain proportion of a population of wildlife will die, mainly to predation and malnutrition. Taking a certain portion of the population, especially of young birds, during the fall will not reduce the resulting population present the following spring. It will merely shift the cause of mortality from natural to human-caused. Obviously, this triggers a whole array of ecological questions, not the least of which is what happens to the predators that might be dependent on the game species. We assumed that these predators could shift to other small things, such as rabbits or rodents. Gambel's quail populations hold up well in the face of fall hunting, and tend to vary in relation to winter precipitation.

As I've mentioned, I preferred fall to spring hunting. Early October, when the fall hunting season traditionally occurs, is the best of all times to be in southwestern forests. Brisk mornings have driven off most of the obnoxious insects. Days are normally warm and still; the sky is brilliant blue. The oak and aspen leaves may have begun to turn. No better time exists to simply loaf in the woods. Contrast this with southwestern springs, which are invariably cold, windy, and impacted by fast-moving and unpredictable snowstorms. Being out at dawn to sit still and hidden during such weather is too much akin to the long mornings in cold turkey blinds, waiting for the birds to decide to come to bait. Give me something a bit balmier.

Also, I've always preferred hunting turkey with a small caliber rifle, rather than a shotgun. This goes counter to the grain of "political correctness" in the turkey hunter ranks.[1] As turkey hunting has become more of a spring event, wherein ardent gobblers are lured by camouflaged human sirens who have mastered the plaintive "tworks" of the hen, the shotgun has become the gun of choice for administering the coup de grâce. Thus the skill in spring hunting lies mostly in learning to call the animal and developing the patience to sit and wait until the gobbler is in shooting range. For me, moving quietly through the woods on a fall day, periodically sitting with my back against a ponderosa pine, listening to the abundant bird life, and watching squirrels, deer, and other forest creatures satisfies whatever atavistic vision I might have had of being a hunter. Carrying a nicely crafted .22 Hornet or .25-20 rifle adds to the fantasy. If a turkey places itself in my sights, that is pure gravy. Under such circumstances, killing a turkey for the table may provide a focus for being in the woods, but not killing one does not constitute failure. Such days are successes the moment they begin. They require nothing more than being there.

Yet, over the years, I have seen fall hunting become less popular and listened to arguments from the hunter ranks to outlaw the use of rifles for turkey hunting. This latter has been justified on the basis of safety—hunters calling turkeys do not feel safe knowing that someone might be creeping around the woods with a rifle. Also, there is some concern that rifle hunters might not find birds that they have wounded more often than shotgun hunters. I don't know if either of these arguments can be justified by real numbers. The last time I checked, Arizona had experienced only one turkey hunter fatality during its entire history, and that hunter was killed with a shotgun.

Anyway, I had always been a devotee of the fall turkey hunt and resisted any changes in its structure. Toward the end of my tenure with the Arizona Game and Fish Department, however, I witnessed a phenomenon that made me wonder about the potentially damaging effects of fall hunting on Merriam's turkey populations—something I had denied through my entire career. While I was periodically helping trap turkeys, we noticed that some of the wintering flocks, especially of hens and poults, were visiting some of our old trap sites, looking for another handout of rolled oats. Some of these sites had not been used for a year or two, yet obviously some of the birds remembered them and checked them out.

This brought me to envision a scenario in which heavy fall hunting of turkeys might depress a turkey population over the long haul. A large percentage of turkeys killed by fall hunters are taken from flocks of hens with poults. More often than not, a hunter seeing such a flock will select for the larger bird, this being the mature hen. By

fall, given adequate food supplies, poults are large enough and experienced enough to survive without the hen, so loss of a hen within a
flock may not be disastrous. However, during years of drought, when
mast (large seed) supplies fail, or during severe winters, when food
supplies are covered with snow and birds are forced below their normal wintering range, the "flock memory" that brought turkeys back
to our deserted bait stations may become critical to survival. A single
old hen, perhaps five or six years in age, that remembers the location
of a particular grove of oaks that was able to produce acorns during a
period of stress, might lead the flock to such a place and make the
difference between survival and death. Similarly, a hen that recalls
an isolated stringer of ponderosa pine reaching down a canyon bottom into winter range that had once provided an emergency supply
of pine seeds, or a warm spring that was lined with green aquatic
plants and perhaps a population of invertebrates, could save a family
flock.

Such an idea, hypothetical at this time, gives the adult flock hens
a renewed value and suggests that protecting the mature birds in fall
flocks might be extremely important.

Another factor now leads me to question fall hunting, at least in
Merriam's turkey populations. Within its native range, the bird does
not nest until it is two years of age. I was first made aware of this
possibility by a young biologist named Dave Lockwood, who was
working for New Mexico Game and Fish about the time I was planning
new turkey research in the 1980s. Dave had begun to successfully radio track turkeys in the Sacramento Mountains of south-central New
Mexico, and he focused his efforts on locating nests and evaluating
their success. He was surprised to notice that virtually none of the
yearling hens were nesting and wrote such in his annual reports. He
was heavily questioned on this, especially by eastern turkey biologists. Yearling hens in the east nest at roughly the same rates as older
hens.

Dave was exonerated by a study we later conducted in the
Chevelon Ranger District (see next chapter), where we also found
the yearling hens failing to nest. Rick Hoffman found similar results

in Colorado. So Merriam's turkeys were different in this regard, at least within most of their historic range. Interestingly enough, yearling Merriam's turkeys in the Black Hills of South Dakota nest regularly. This is a population that was established by bringing in birds from New Mexico and Colorado about 1950. It has done extremely well. Non-nesting of Merriam's yearlings, then, is not inherited. It is undoubtedly related to the relatively poor overall nutritional quality of the southwestern turkey ranges—an indication that the birds are perhaps surviving under a certain amount of stress at all times.

I drew a certain satisfaction from our data when it began to support Dave Lockwood's findings, and I felt that we had perhaps been involved in discovering something new about turkey biology. Then one day I was reading back through J. Stokely Ligon's 1946 monograph on Merriam's turkeys and found the simple statement, buried deeply in a paragraph on turkey nesting, that Merriam's turkey yearling hens do not nest. Ligon had figured it out forty years earlier, without the help of radio-marked hens. Oh, well!

But back to the implications of this on fall hunting. If some selection of mature hens occurs during the fall hunt, then a proportion of the hen population that will be able to reproduce the following spring has been removed. The disproportionate number of yearling hens that are left will simply not get the job done. So unless fall hunters can be trained not to shoot mature hens, perhaps fall hunting is open to question.

This, of course, is all hypothetical. What we may need (I humbly concede), now that we have a legitimate hypothesis to test, is a study of the effects of fall hunting on the ability of the population to survive the winter.

11 A Knickerbocker's Tale

About 1985, I again found myself involved with turkeys. The minimal habitat work on the South Rim study had long since been completed, although the graduate student we hired never managed to write a thesis. In 1976 I finally completed a report that summarized his data. but I was too busy to try to publish it. It lies hidden somewhere in the Game and Fish Department federal aid files.

Of the fifteen years that I had been away from turkey research, eight were spent in intensive studies of mountain lions in relatively remote settings. I had little contact with the issues surrounding other species of wildlife and their habitat, and I paid little attention to the inner workings of the game department. I felt like Washington Irving's Rip Van Winkle coming back to civilization. My desire was simply to be left alone to get the research on lions done as well as I could. In fact, the lion work placed me in close contact with people in other walks of life: ranchers, loggers, guides, and environmental activists. My closest acquaintances were people in small rural communities, many deriving their living from the land. The more I worked with these people, the more I learned to respect their abilities, even though I didn't always agree with their attitudes toward wildlife.

I was still concerned about turkeys. I felt that serious problems still existed over long-term habitat modification as a result of extensive even-aged timber management on the Mogollon Rim. In spite of the efforts of Fred Phillips and others like him, the game department simply did not have enough objective information to challenge the Forest Service over the nuances of timber management policies.

Fred had continued to be a key player in turkey management

throughout the time that our formal turkey research was suspended, and he was instrumental in setting studies in motion once again. He had fought the Forest Service to a standstill over turkey roosts, the only element of turkey habitat for which we had relatively clear data. However, everyone involved with Merriam's turkeys, especially Fred, was painfully aware that turkeys do not live by roosts alone. Through the 1970s and into the 1980s, as the conversion of the forest to young, evenly spaced trees continued, turkey numbers seemed to decrease. Roadside survey and hunt data suggested a long-term decline, but such data are subject to many uncontrolled forces. Nonetheless, by 1983, wildlife managers in Arizona were becoming worried about turkeys, and Fred once again led the way. In 1985, he organized a turkey workshop in Williams to assess the problems of turkey management and to bring about some kind of action. By this time, because of his successes at challenging Forest Service timber policies, Fred was known by turkey biologists across the United States, and he invited turkey specialists to participate in the workshop from as far as Missouri, Pennsylvania, and South Carolina. Forest Service biologists from the regional office in Albuquerque attended. Arizona Game and Fish Department division chiefs from Phoenix attended. In two days of intense discussion, this group created important recommendations for future turkey management and turkey research. I compiled the results into a report that formed the basis, at last, for a study of turkey habitat requirements and causes of mortality.

The above workshop delineated our general objectives for turkey research, and I began to work on a study design. Partly because of the success of Fred's workshop, I requested an advisory group to help select an appropriate study area and to periodically review our progress to be sure that those of us narrowly involved in research were not allowing our personal interests to lead the study astray. During my career in research, I frequently heard our research biologists accused of isolationism. Research activities in the Arizona Game and Fish Department were not viewed as being responsive to the needs of wildlife managers in the field. I agreed with this point of view, but blamed it on the administration's use of research to fight political flash fires rather than on any aloofness within our branch. Until we could sustain long-term research and be given time to implement findings, the problems would remain.

Because of this, and because I now felt a strong need to build a base of support for any new study, I suggested a committee to be made up of people in positions destined to apply our results. Such people would be, mainly, regional biologists and district wildlife managers with turkey management responsibilities. My first choice for such a committee included, of course, Fred Phillips. The group we assembled initially functioned well. At its first meeting, it selected the new turkey study area. This wasn't accomplished without some disagreement, because each member of the group represented a particular area and particular problem in turkey management. By the end of the second day, however, a consensus was reached, with all agreeing that the Chevelon Ranger District, located centrally in Arizona's turkey habitat, represented a reasonable compromise, both in terms of location and suitability for addressing the questions. With a study area selected, we were able to begin to develop a detailed study plan. By the winter of 1985-86, we were ready to study turkey habitat in Arizona.

By this time my old partner, Miles, had long since gone back to Montana. Arizona had proven too tame, and the bureaucracy too inconstant for his cowboy upbringing. Other things had changed as well. The environmental surge of the 1970s had created a surplus of young people with degrees in biology or wildlife management. Where we once hired assistants such as Miles for our projects from the ranks of cowboys, trappers, and others with practical field experience, we now hired technicians with bachelor's or master's degrees. An assistant's job was not a career; it was an entry point. You could not hope to train and retain field-workers for the duration of a project. Nonetheless, these young assistants were highly motivated, learned quickly, and often brought new and innovative ideas to the project.

Radio-tracking equipment was now reliable. Successful tracking of turkeys was assured. Also, the personal computer was now a standard tool, with user-friendly databases, spreadsheets, and statistical software becoming increasingly common. When I had left turkey habitat research fifteen years before, we were still analyzing data with desktop calculators. The amount of data we could handle was extremely limited. When I returned to turkey research, tools were available that allowed us to gather and record many hundreds of times more information than had been possible during the early studies. We could also perform analysis and modeling tasks in a few seconds that had been completely beyond the capabilities of our primitive calculators. While I had experience in radio-tracking equipment, and had bought my own personal computer as early as user-friendly units became available, I nonetheless felt behind the times technologically.

Even in trapping turkeys, things had changed. The tool of choice was a drop net that was much easier on the birds. Fred Phillips had been instrumental in developing this new technique. We were lucky to start the project with two extremely capable field men, Jim Wegge and Ron Day, and the first winter's trapping went well, with some fifty birds captured and fitted with radios. It was hard for me to believe that we actually had fifty radio-marked turkeys in the woods being located regularly and providing data on habitat, movements, and mortality. We had, twenty years earlier, labored to merely get one or two radios that would work for a few weeks; we now expected most of these units to function for two to three years, assuming the turkey survived that long. Not only that, if we failed to find a radio-marked bird on a given day, a call to Phoenix would direct the department's airplane over the area. An experienced radio tracker, usually Bill Carrell from our Phoenix research laboratory, called locations of missing birds to us from the air. We had merely to gather data.

But this created new problems. Once we had radio-marked birds, we needed a clear plan of what we intended to do with them. What data should we gather? How should it be analyzed? For all the years we spent trying to develop good radio-tracking equipment, we now realized that this was just the beginning. In assessing habitat for turkeys, we had assumed that some ideal condition existed that would provide the optimum quantity and dispersion of the various food and cover elements the species requires. We also assumed that the species would instinctively recognize this optimum condition and would feel most comfortable when residing within it, that it would feel less secure in inferior habitats and adjust accordingly.

During our earlier observational work on the Moqui, we had developed the basics of habitat measurement. We had proceeded there on the assumption that, if we observed an undisturbed flock of turkeys at a given point, then the habitat around that point could be considered acceptable to the birds. If we measured habitat characteristics at enough points and also made the same measurements on a larger sample representing the range of conditions over the entire study area, we should be able to begin to understand the habitat elements that turkeys were using in excess of their availability.

Before radio-tracking studies were possible, awareness of the subtleties of habitat selection came slowly and sometimes from unexpected sources. We learned early that turkeys were not necessarily creatures of simple behavior, and that different ages or sexes of turkeys required different habitat elements at times. Our learning process was often a bit embarrassing.

I remember trapping birds to send to California during the winter of 1965, shortly after I began to work with turkeys. I had buried myself in turkey literature, but still had much to learn. We baited birds for the transplant on a traditional wintering area south of Flagstaff. The California Department of Fish and Game, obviously better funded than Arizona's department, sent a pair of biologists over in a twin-engine airplane to fly the birds back, so we wanted to catch birds as quickly as possible. All went reasonably well, and we made two successful shots of the net in one morning, catching thirty-two turkeys. These were mostly juveniles hatched the preceding spring. As we removed the birds from the net and crated them, I puzzled over the sex of the immature birds, and wondered why I could not clearly pick out males. The adult hens were easy to classify. There were obviously no big gobblers in the net, but I commented several times that some of the younger birds *had* to be males.

Only after we shipped the birds, and I once again reviewed the texts for better information on sex determination on seven- to eight-month-old turkeys, did I learn that male and female poults tend to segregate by late winter. The young females stay with adult hens; the young males wander off in sibling groups and, possibly, join mature gobblers. I therefore have no doubt, in retrospect, that California received only female birds from that shipment. I can only hope that they were planted in an area where mature males were already present. If not, the transplant failed.

The greater lesson here was that the social behavior of turkeys may affect their habitat needs. Gobblers were simply not feeding at the site where we trapped the above birds. We had observed differences in habitat selected by gobblers and hens with poults during our South Rim study, but a detailed study of the significance of such habitat partitioning has yet to be made. Radio tracking of turkeys has revealed clearly that habitat requirements change with social or nutritional requirements, which vary greatly over the course of a year. Habitat can only be discussed in association with these seasonal requirements. For some of these aspects of habitat selection behavior, we know much; for others, we still have little solid information. The problems associated with studying the birds, along with the methods used, vary with the time of year and the behavior of the birds involved.

Radio tracking allowed us to locate turkeys at all times of day or night and find out what they were doing. We could then classify habitat based on specific forms of behavior, including winter feeding habitats, winter roosts, movement corridors between winter and summer ranges, spring breeding habitats, nesting habitats, brood-rearing habitats (which change as broods grow), summer roosts, and summer and fall feeding and loafing habitats. We could differentiate the habitat requirements of different age-classes of birds, different sexes, and birds of different reproductive status (such as hens with or without young).

Habitat research, then, required more than just locating turkeys and plotting their movements on a map. We needed to know the structural and nutritional components of the habitats the birds were using, the way these components were used, and how they interrelated. On the Moqui study, fifteen years earlier, we had conceptualized a sample unit of habitat to be measured around a point. We assumed that turkeys were reacting to visual stimuli in the areas they moved through.

The boundaries of areas to be measured were determined by what we called the visual horizontal cover distance around the central point of the site. The visual horizontal distance was defined as the distance a turkey would be likely to see movement from that central point. We therefore squatted to lower our eyes to the approximate height of a turkey's head and looked around. More specifically, we measured the distance we could see along four randomly chosen radials from the site center. We normally selected a tree or other landmark at approximately the maximum visibility distance along a radial, then paced the distance to it. Measurements of other site characteristics were made systematically as we returned to the center point.

Whatever technique is used to make the measurements, this visual horizontal distance defines the outer boundaries of the site to be characterized. Once that is determined, additional measurements are made of tree canopy cover, shrub cover, and herbaceous ground cover within the visible radius. These basic measurements are taken, regardless of the season of use or behavior of turkeys on the site. Overstory is important for shade, protection from precipitation, a more abstract characteristic called thermal cover, and protection from avian predators. It also provides trees to fly into to escape terrestrial predators. Horizontal cover provides protection from wind (another aspect of thermal cover) and places to hide from both terrestrial and avian predators. Herbaceous ground cover generally is of value for food, including the invertebrates it attracts, and it may also be important as escape or hiding cover, especially for poults.

The techniques used for measuring habitat characteristics are varied, and different workers have used different approaches. Methods have not yet been standardized, perhaps cannot be, but books have been written on the subject. A discussion of techniques would be too long and tedious for this publication, but, based upon such measurements, biologists are beginning to be able to describe the selected habitats for the above behavioral classes. These habitat needs can be followed through the turkey year. Perhaps the easiest way to discuss this habitat selection behavior is to follow the birds through a turkey year, starting with winter.

12 It's a Long, Long Time from December to May

Before about 1985, winter habitat of Merriam's turkey, with the exception of roosts, had not received much study. This was due, in part, to the fact that winter is normally turkey trapping time, and personnel assigned to studies had little opportunity to carry on other activities. In addition to this, habitat elements that were suspected of being more limiting to birds, such as nest sites or brood-rearing areas, received most research effort, and these are spring and summer behaviors. Finally, studying Merriam's turkey on winter range can be frustrating. Although the Flagstaff area is cold during the winter because of its high elevation, it is still in the sunny Southwest, so slushy snow and mud are the norm, making access to many wintering areas difficult. The nighttime freezing and midday thawing typical of this area limit the utility of snow machines. The mud and the large areas involved often made snowshoes or skis ineffective.

There were many days during our earlier efforts when we spent more time digging our vehicles out than we did observing turkeys. Perhaps the most memorable was a trip I made during early spring to the Moqui to disassemble one of the box traps. I drove into the area on frozen ground, parked my vehicle about fifty yards from the trap, which was as close as I could get, then proceeded to haul the trap out a panel at a time. With all the huffing and puffing and rest stops needed to drag the panels through the eighteen-inch snow, I spent at least two hours getting the pieces on the truck. On my final trip, I realized as I approached the vehicle that the ground under it had thawed. The pickup had simply sunk in place. All four wheels were axle-deep in mud.

I was in a spot where radio contact was impossible. It would have done little good anyway, because no one could reach me until the ground solidified with the next night's freeze, which I could only hope would happen—it was late enough in the year that even a light cloud cover would have prevented a frost. I spent the remainder of the day jacking the truck up and filling the holes under the tires with brush and tree limbs. There were no rocks in the immediate vicinity. By dark, I had succeeded in turning the vehicle completely around by lifting it then pushing it sidewise off of the jack. However, I hadn't moved it three feet homeward. Every time I moved it off one of my constructed brush piles, it sunk again to its axles and drive shaft.

Finally, at dark, I walked a short distance to a deserted cabin and built a fire in its tumbledown fireplace. The rotted remains of a couch, covered with rat droppings, provided a bed. I alternated dozing with rising to warm myself by the fire and step outside to check the condition of the ground and sky. The sky remained clear, but the ground did not freeze until after 2 A.M. Once the mud had again solidified, I started the truck, put it in gear, and drove home.

Study difficulties aside, knowledge of winter habitat requirements is now attaining high priority in turkey research. Good radio-tracking equipment, better snow vehicles, and easy access to aircraft for aerial locations have made winter studies more possible. Winter is undoubtedly a stressful period for many populations of Merriam's turkeys, due mainly to limited availability of food. Hence, to understand selection of habitat by turkeys on winter range, we must also understand their nutritional needs. Failing food supplies may force birds to use areas that would be unacceptable if food was abundant.

Winter range typically includes suitable roost sites, surrounded by areas supporting a diversity of food-producing plant species, allowing the birds to forage without undue travel or exposure to predation. In most southwestern winter habitats, food is probably more limiting than cover. During some winters, suitable food in the form of acorns, grass seed heads, or pine seeds may be absent. Where thick stands of piñon-juniper woodlands surround ponderosa pine roosts, or where shrubs encroach as an understory to woodland or pine forests, cover can actually be too dense. Turkeys rely on their sharp eyes to detect predators, and on their legs and wings to escape. Cover dense enough to limit their vision and restrict their movements increases their vulnerability to predation by coyotes, fox, bobcats, and mountain lions, all of which are fond of turkey meat.

In terms of feeding behavior, turkeys at all seasons are feathered ruminants. With their large crops, they can rapidly gather many seeds, then retire to the safety of suitable loafing areas to digest the food. (One crop that I know of held over six hundred piñon nuts when the bird was killed by a hunter.) This adaptation minimizes the time the bird is exposed while feeding. However, turkeys must compete for food with a large array of other wild and domestic species. The mast (large seed) species that they favor during fall and winter (ponderosa pine seed, Gambel oak acorns, and piñon nuts) are eaten in the tree by many insects, birds, and mammals. Such heavy use of mast before it falls to the ground, added to the vagaries of seed production for these species, makes its availability to turkeys uncertain at best. Because turkeys are mainly ground foragers, they are forced to exist on leftovers for much of their fall and winter food.

And the same processes continue on the ground, perhaps at an accelerated rate. Many of the same species that take seeds in the trees certainly follow them to the ground. Both tree and ground squirrels take seeds of all kinds. A large assortment of other ground-dwelling rodents, such as wood rats and mice, gather the seeds. Jays, crows, and ravens feed heavily on piñon nuts. Clark's nutcrackers fly down from roosts on mountains a great distance away and gather seeds to carry back to the high country. Also on the ground, larger mammals enter the scene. Deer, elk, javelina, bears, and cattle eat acorns and piñon nuts.

Added to the problems of competition, mast crops are not reliable in southwestern forests. During some years, acorn and pine seed crops may fail entirely. Grass seeds, juniper berries, and buds of trees and shrubs may at times be the only available foods. Where high densities of elk and cattle share the winter range with turkeys, grass seed heads may be grazed off by early fall. Competition by other birds and rodents for buds on shrubs and low-hanging trees may be acute.

If the winter food supply is depleted in areas with suitable roosts and protective cover, turkeys are forced to range farther from winter roosts and into poor habitat. This places them at higher risk to both mammalian predators and to raptors. Coyotes become especially adroit at taking the birds and will literally live with the large winter flocks, picking off birds that make mistakes. Bobcats and foxes perhaps contribute less to turkey mortality, but they are inclined to stalk or lie in wait in denser cover. Thus in late winter, turkeys may become more vulnerable to predation at the very time that they are in the poorest physiological condition. Predation rates definitely increase during late winter and early spring, before green forage is available in more suitable habitats. When all of this is considered, one wonders how turkeys survive winter at all. In many places, in many years, populations drop to drastically low levels by spring.

Food availability and quality during winter months affect turkey numbers in at least one other way—by delimiting the production of young. As mentioned previously, studies in Arizona and New Mexico have disclosed an almost total failure of yearling hens to nest. This is apparently due to poor nutrition in southwestern populations. Nesting of yearling birds is more common in the eastern subspecies. And, in the Black Hills of South Dakota, where Merriam's turkeys have been transplanted, yearlings nest at rates similar to adults. The Black Hills differ from the southwest in having more consistent production of ponderosa pine seeds, earlier availability of green forage in spring, and in some areas, access to grain fields and feedlots. From all appearances, the nutritional regime available on many southwestern turkey ranges simply does not prepare young turkeys for nesting. Such a lack of nesting by yearlings might reduce potential annual productivity of the population by thirty percent or more. This phenomenon may also suggest that the Merriam's turkey is for some reason not perfectly adapted to what we have heretofore considered its "native" range.

Winter roosts are in some ways the most studied aspect of turkey habitat, but from a sociological perspective, they are the least understood. From all appearances, turkey behavior at winter roost sites seems designed to increase mortality in every possible way. Sitting in exposed treetops through the intense snowfall and heavy winds of mountain storms, as opposed to sleeping in clusters on the ground as some quail do or using dense canopies of low piñons or junipers in protected canyons, seems to be extremely wasteful of energy. One must assume that avoidance of predators has had greater adaptive value than avoidance of the elements.

But even in the simple act of entering roosts, especially winter roosts, turkeys seem to work against themselves in avoiding predators. Few things in the woods are noisier than turkeys going to bed. Considering that winter roost sites may be the congregating points for two hundred or more turkeys in some areas, "tworking" turkeys, loudly announcing their immediate plans to retire, can set up quite a cacophony. And they start while still on the ground. Nothing seems of less adaptive value than congregating in large groups at dusk, when predators have an advantage for stalking, announcing loudly your location, flapping into treetops, and rustling around from tree to tree until you are comfortable, all the while continuing to vocalize your plans to the world. Any coyote that didn't score at bedtime would probably be wise enough to wait around for morning. Every predator in the woods, whether bobcat, puma, coyote, fox, owl, or eagle, must know the location of the nearest winter roost.

Yet we must look for adaptive values in any form of behavior to understand the species and its habitat needs. Some selective pressure over the ages must have resulted in the evolution of roosting behavior, and it must provide some kind of survival advantage. But, with our present knowledge, its value is extremely difficult to envision. Maybe the ruckus at bedtime is a means of assembling all groups to the roost—just making sure that no one is lost. If turkeys regularly drifted from roost to roost, using new sites each night at random, this idea might make sense. However, this is not the norm for roosting in winter. Wintering birds tend to use one or two traditional roosts near good feeding areas. Many of these roosts are used for decades. Certainly all turkeys using them know their location. Most flocks include older birds that have wintered in the area before. Assembly calls seem unnecessary.

One hypothesis regarding such vocalizing at roosts is that it involves actual communication of the day's activities. Berndt Heinrich, for example, found that ravens communicate information regarding food sources to other ravens at communal roosts. The large winter roosts of turkeys frequently involve several flocks that separate during the day, each feeding in a different direction. Perhaps they do compare notes at the end of the day, but so far no one has been able to provide such an orderly reason for their pre-slumber revelry.

We might hypothesize that large winter roost sites occur as a result of limited winter food supplies. Perhaps turkeys do not congregate when food is more abundant and can shift roosts more frequently. Announcing, "we're using *this* roost tonight" might make sense under such circumstances. When food becomes scarce, such assembly call behavior becomes maladaptive. Turkey biologists working in areas where food is abundant do not seem to be as concerned with roost site quality as are southwestern biologists working with Merriam's. Maybe there is a message here.

But why would a large bird choose to roost high in trees in the first place rather than clustering on the ground like bobwhites? At least one authority on sleeping birds has noted that ground-nesting birds tend also to roost on the ground; tree nesting birds roost in trees. Turkeys nest on the ground, so they certainly violate this rule. Another authority, specializing in gallinaceous bird behavior, suggests that this behavior is strictly a function of size—large ungainly birds must roost away from terrestrial predators simply because they are not fast enough to escape (as, presumably, are the smaller quail). I'm not sure I buy this entirely. Sage grouse, for example, roost in scattered assemblages on the ground, and they are far from nimble. I've netted a good many of them before they could get airborne and have plucked a few out of the air with a net after they took wing. Admittedly, trees are not common in sage grouse country, but many riparian areas with conifers, cottonwoods, willows, or sycamores do occur in drainages, so adaptation to roosting in trees for the sage grouse does not seem to have been an impossible evolutionary option. Presumably, size should have pushed sage grouse as well as turkeys in that direction.

Whatever the case, suitable roosts surrounded by areas with adequate food constitute turkey winter habitat. Poor roost sites increase vulnerability to predators. Lack of food forces birds to range further, feed longer in exposed situations, or abandon good roost sites for ones where, again, vulnerability to predators increases. Mingled with these winter habitats are loafing areas—warm hillsides where the birds can rest midday and digest food. I find it interesting that turkeys rarely fly into trees for midday snoozes but rather hang out on the ground, usually in places where surrounding terrain is fairly open, allowing the birds to see an approaching predator. They tend to slip quietly into these daytime napping sites, without any of the fanfare involved in going to bed at night. One or more birds of a flock seem always to be on watch, often from a slightly elevated perch on the limbs of a downed tree. More often than not, such sites are also located near the crest of a slope, giving the birds an open route to launch themselves quietly and fly rapidly downhill when threatened.

13 It's Spring Again

The transition from winter to spring and summer is one of immense activity for Merriam's turkeys. In their mountainous range, winter and summer habitats may be far apart. As noted earlier, seasonal movements up to forty miles have been documented in Arizona. Merriam's turkeys have been described by some as migratory, but no real pattern of migration exists. The birds probably move within suitable broad expanses of habitat to areas with the best food supplies. If this assumes a pattern over time, it may be due to the passing of a flock memory from generation to generation. In some areas, birds do not need to move long distances between seasons, but merely shift locally to areas with suitable foods.

Over most of the Southwest, birds will begin their gradual move upward in elevation in late March or April, more or less following the snow line and associated new growth of grasses and other herbaceous plants. Breeding activity begins about this time on the winter range and continues on to the summer range. In one sense, breeding behavior is the best known element of turkey activity. Thousands of hunters annually apply their knowledge of the tom's strutting behavior to shoot a bird for the table. Spring gobbler hunting has become ritualized to the point that it is without doubt the most singularly "American" form of the hunting sports. A major industry produces dozens of varieties of calls, an infinite range of camouflage patterns for clothes and blinds, tree stands, specialized shotguns, guides, lodges, and trinkets, all for the turkey hunter. Regardless of the political decision of our founding fathers, Ben Franklin in reality had his way. Revenues spent on turkey hunting and turkey management exceed by many times any dollars spent on the bald eagle. And 90 percent of this expenditure is because tom turkeys strut and come to a call.

Interestingly, this best known and almost symbolic aspect of turkey behavior—strutting—is the least researched by scientists. The gobbler, whose role in reproduction is a short period of huffing, puffing, and breeding, has largely been ignored, mainly because males willing to breed are rarely in short supply. But the behavior of the breeding male (and for that matter, attendant females) is somewhat unique in the world of birds and worthy of attention. For one thing, the species does not appear to form breeding territories as is so common in most songbirds and, in modified forms, even in species more closely related to turkeys. Most of the grouse, for example, perform their breeding rites on established sites. Sage grouse and the prairie grouse species assemble on traditional leks (breeding grounds) that are used for decades. Forest grouse do their drumming on established logs. But turkeys gobble and carry on while drifting over considerable acreage. Their territory, if it exists, shifts with them and is perhaps determined only by the radius over which other breeding birds can hear their gobbling.

Starting at daybreak, this nuptial procession will happen anywhere reasonably open forest conditions exist, presumably so that the bird can be seen for a suitable distance when strutting. It is a common spring phenomenon in wild turkey country, but little is known about the habitat or nutritional needs of the breeding males during midday hours when breeding activity subsides. Similarly, the behavior of hens moving to and away from these strutting toms has been given little attention. Because all hens of reproductive age seem to breed (or at least a high percentage do), we assume that habitat during the breeding season is one of the least limiting. Nonetheless, there is much to be learned about the breeding activities in turkeys and how they function to maintain suitable genetic diversity in wild populations. And because of all the noise, we would expect breeding birds to be particularly susceptible to predation.

Once bred, turkey hens handle all the work of reproduction alone.

Male turkeys are the ultimate playboys, having a spring fling with multiple females, then spending the rest of the year lounging about the woods with the boys, with no responsibility other than filling their crops. They don't even hang around to defend the nest. They are truly a lazy lot and perhaps deserve to be zapped by a shotgun at the peak of their ardor. Maybe it's a form of subconscious envy that brings the human male to pursue the turkey gobbler.

By about mid-May, the female starts laying eggs. This is usually in a well-hidden site, although the quality of nest sites chosen varies considerably. Some hens lay their eggs in the open. Before the advent of radio tracking, the poorer nest sites were the ones most often found by people working in the woods. As a result, early turkey biologists probably had a distorted view of nesting habitat and may have protected the wrong kind of sites.

Because of concern over nesting habitat, turkey-nesting behavior was studied soon after good radio-tracking equipment became available. Once located, nests provide specific points for making habitat measurements. Characterization of nest sites began to yield solid, discrete data, and we now know perhaps as much about turkey nesting habitat as we do about habitats required for other activities.

Among turkey biologists, locating nesting hens without disturbing them is considered a special skill. Anyone who has participated in this activity can tell stories of hours spent carefully searching an area from which a radio beep emanated, only to discover too late that they have spooked the nesting bird. It is difficult to believe that a creature as large as a turkey hen can hide so well. Fortunately, hens well along in incubation—birds having been on a nest for two weeks or more—do not dislodge easily, so with careful timing, biologists can locate nests without causing hens to abandon them.

Even so, nest searching requires patience. Spending a full workday locating a single nest is not unusual. Locating two nests in a day is an accomplishment. More than that is considered a super feat. If you are monitoring fifty potential nesting hens, locating all nests at exactly the right time to avoid abandonment can be an all-consuming springtime occupation for a field biologist.

Nest searches begin when the signal from a radio-tagged hen fails to change location for a week or more. If you are a quarter mile or greater from the marked animal, determining the general direction from which a signal emanates is relatively easy. As you move closer, the signal becomes stronger, and directionality wanes. Even though modern radio-tracking receivers are fitted with adjustments that attenuate the signal, and better antennas have been slowly developed, determining the actual direction of the signal source at very close range (say under fifty yards) becomes an art. Your radio signal ultimately shifts from a somewhat variable, melodic beep to a loud, constant thump that does not change, no matter which way you point your directional antenna.

Workers very quickly learn to use a variety of homespun techniques to facilitate locating radio-marked animals close in. These include screening the receiver's antenna with your body while turning slowly in a circle and listening for subtle signal changes; walking behind trees, large rocks, or other terrain features to weaken the signal; even removing the antenna and using tiny substitutes, such as a pocket knife blade or hand-formed paper clip. Such finessing can make the difference between inadvertently flushing a hen and spotting her on her nest and leaving her undisturbed.

Once an observer has followed the signal to the point of antenna saturation, caution is the key to success. If you do not know with certainty the direction of the nest, you don't move. If you do know, you scan, usually with binoculars, all potential nest sites in your range of vision. The goal is not to approach without being detected—the hen undoubtedly knows you are there—but rather to identify the nest site and leave the hen thinking that she has not been detected. A flushed hen is a failure as far as a nest-searcher is concerned. Research can be intrusive enough without actually reducing productivity of a population through clumsy technique.

So you scan carefully, inspecting every vegetative clump near bases of trees or against rock outcrops, slash piles, fallen trees, limbs, or anything creating a place to hide a nest. You scan every inch of potential habitat in the direction of the signal, then sit a while and scan again. If your initial search ultimately reveals no bird, you move, but not directly toward the signal source. You circle at an angle that may bring you slightly, but not much, closer. Once you have moved enough (perhaps fifteen to twenty yards), you again stop and take a reading. This "triangulation" refines your intuitive sense of where the nest may be. You now have two intersecting lines that cross roughly in an ill-defined area, still with several potential sites. Once again you scan, taking as much as an hour to peer into every small opening in the vegetation.

During all of this process, you are not looking for a turkey. What you hope to see is perhaps the outline of an eye (about one-fourth inch in diameter) peering back at you from some small break in the vegetation. Or you may notice a series of striations that are not quite like the surrounding twigs and realize that you have discovered the tip of a wing feather with black and white pigments. At times you will sense a larger, more solid, elliptical form deep in a shadow that is the entire body of a crouched hen.

If the second stop produces no nest, you move again, this time more carefully and a shorter distance, for you are certainly closer, and the bird is watching you. You stop and scan again, using another radio triangulation, if possible, to narrow the area to be searched. Even with such careful technique, you are at times fooled by nature or by errant turkeys in this process of searching. Your greatest enemy is the bundle of expectations that you bring with you to the site. On one of my first nest-locating efforts, for example, I hiked into a steep canyon on the Apache-Sitgreaves National Forest. The radio signal from the hen I was seeking had not moved for almost three weeks, and hence she was believed to be safe to approach. Reaching the point where my signal had begun to saturate was not difficult. My antenna pointed across a small canyon to a steep slope covered with mid-sized (eight- to twelve-inch trunk diameter) ponderosa pine and Douglas fir. The understory vegetation was not dense, but dead limbs and fallen stems of smaller trees were scattered over the hillside. I scanned carefully, with little hope of seeing the bird. After some fifteen minutes, I shifted laterally to get closer and triangulate. This led me across the canyon into a small, rocky drainage, which I found strewn with turkey feathers. A quick check of a breast feather told me that this had been a hen. I immediately assumed that I was dealing with a dead, rather than nesting, turkey, and I shifted my attention to determining the cause of mortality. Flushing the bird was no longer a matter of concern.

But I failed to register sign that indicated that this kill had probably occurred prior to the time the radio-tagged bird had settled in the area. The feathers were weathered and obviously had lain on the ground through at least one snowfall. Some had many conifer needles on top of them, suggesting they had been lying on the slope for a month or more. Nonetheless, feeling confident that I had found the radio-marked turkey's remains, I searched the hillside without caution. A couple of narrow scrape marks in the forest litter within about fifteen yards and one small, but weathered hump where something might earlier have been temporarily covered convinced me that a bobcat was probably the culprit.

Once I had satisfied myself that I had done my best on determining the cause of death, I shifted my search to the transmitter. It was not to be found near the mortality site. I searched across the area, took readings on the receiver, and gridded the area again. I looked in holes under rocks and kicked through vegetation where the unit might have been buried. The tight quarters of the canyon created signal bounce that frustrated efforts at such close-range location. Finally, I began to search a larger area. The steepness of the slope (my inclinometer gave it an average of 70 percent) forced me to bring my binoculars once again into play, hoping that I could spot the tiny radio package in the conifer needles without scrambling over every inch of the hillside. As I scanned past a clump of slash at the base of a pole-sized pine, I sensed a smoothly curved object with about a four-inch radius. A single round circle some one-fourth inch in diameter subtended this curve. I did a double take. About fifteen yards away, quite alive, was the nesting hen I had come to find. I could see only the top of her head and one eye peering over the brush. I had been all around her. She was a tolerant lady.

I described the site location, so that habitat analysis could be made after the eggs hatched and slipped away as quietly as I could, feeling decidedly foolish about my general insensitivity to sign. On paper the day was a success—an undisturbed nesting hen *and* a documented natural mortality. In reality, I knew I had done a lousy job.

A briefer example illustrates other subtleties of nest finding. On this day, the signal was coming from a relatively open hillside (an old burned area) immediately adjacent to one of the major graded forest roads in the area. At least thirty cars a day traveled this road. The signal was almost saturated at the point I left my pickup, and I knew that I was within fifty yards of the bird. My initial reading gave me a line straight toward one of the few clumps of young Gambel oak sprouting on the hillside. Old slash and relatively tall grass surrounded it. This undoubtedly would be an easy search. There was only one suitable nest site in view. I circled slightly to the left and drew closer. My second reading confirmed proximity of the signal to the oak clump, and I considered my job as good as done. If possible, however, I wanted to see the bird. A ridge on the far side of the nest might give a view downward into the low cluster of oak, so I circled the site at some fifteen yards, periodically peering into the foliage with my binoculars. Even though the oak clump was relatively sparse, I saw no telltale eye, curve, or pattern.

The ridge provided a good view almost vertically into the site, but a thorough glassing still did not disclose the nest. However, the signal had reversed its direction as I circled the clump, giving support to my initial interpretation. I started back across the shallow drainage to the pickup, passing the oak clump on the remaining side just in case I might catch a glimpse of the bird from there. On what would be my final stop, I realized that I had been so totally fixed on this oak thicket that I had failed to scan any of the surrounding area, so I took time to enlarge my field of search. Almost instantly, I saw a turkey hen sitting in full view alongside a single oak sapling about twenty feet uphill from the oak thicket. The sapling was less than an inch in diameter and less than three feet high, yet the bird had "backed up" a nest with it and was calmly watching me from a cluster of short grass at its base. On my initial approach, I had walked within ten yards of it, but my fixation on the more likely site had prevented me from looking around. Once more humiliated, I described the area for future measurement and stole back to my vehicle. Again, success on paper and success in my mind were two different things. Other biologists have spent much more time than I locating nests, and I suspect that their confessions, too, would provide entertainment.

While nest sites vary in location and habitat selected, and a few deviate significantly from the norm, location of literally hundreds of nests by biologists in several states have revealed a pattern that provides an image of the "ideal." More often than not, nests occur on relatively steep slopes, but in areas where steep terrain is absent, birds will use available sites. In Arizona we have found most nests on slopes ranging from 30 to 70 percent. I find it interesting that such steep terrain is seldom used for other activities by turkeys, such as feeding or loafing. Only when nesting do turkeys reside for extended periods in relatively dense cover on steeper slopes. Some observers have suggested that these steep slopes are the only areas where stands of unlogged old-growth timber still exist, hence are preferred for nesting. This hypothesis has not been tested and may provide a partial explanation. However, I suspect that terrain plays a role in the suitability of nest sites, apart from logging history. Most nests we have observed are backed up against some solid entity. On more level terrain, this may be the bole of a large pine or fir, a dense clump of oak, or a large rock. Steep hillsides, however, with rock outcrops and ledges, provide a superabundance of backdrops for nests. And turkeys use such sites.

Equally as important as the backdrop is relatively low cover on the remaining sides of the nest. Birds prefer to be able to see out, presumably to spot approaching predators without being seen. I suspect that a nest site on a slope has an advantage over one on level ground. A stalking predator would find undetected approach up a hill difficult, and any final rush to the prey would be from a position of disadvantage. A tree or rock outcrop on the uphill side prevents approach from that direction. Another common structural element is dense overhead cover, usually hanging within three to four feet of the nest.

Thus the ideal turkey nest is a cubby, with complete protection from one side, low cover on the others, and a ceiling to eliminate the dangers of aerial attack. Even so, nest predation happens frequently. Studies in Arizona disclosed that setting hens had the highest rate of mortality of any birds over one year of age. (Only very young poults, which disappear from broods at a rapid rate during their first few weeks, suffer higher mortality.)

Obviously, if habitats were modified in a manner that reduces availability of good nesting sites, this hen mortality would be even greater and could affect the turkey population over time. However, in most of the western turkey ranges, relatively dense forest and shrub stands on steep slopes are common, even where the areas are otherwise heavily logged. Nesting site availability is probably one of the least limiting of turkey habitat needs under current conditions, and only extreme thinning, clear-cutting, or forest fires over large areas are likely to affect this. Retaining good cover on steep slopes is probably enough. The turkeys will do the rest.

14 Summertime

By mid-June, most of the eggs have hatched, and the hens have moved their broods of poults to areas where they are most likely to survive. Staying with radio-marked nesting hens is a natural progression of turkey research, and brood habitat requirements have now been fairly well studied. If nest-locators are the masters of wild turkey science, students of brood habitat must be Ph.D.s. Any hunter can tell you how difficult turkeys are to stalk. Virtually every turkey hunting technique incorporates calling or stand hunting, methods in which the turkey comes to the camouflaged and immobile hunter. Hence approaching and observing undisturbed wild birds, even radio-marked ones, seems unlikely, but a few biologists have accomplished it. A few biologists have also let newly hatched turkeys imprint on them, and then wandered the woods with them in the role of a surrogate mother hen. I know of no such imprinting studies that have been carried out on Merriam's turkeys.

To document brood habitat, observers must be able to confirm that a particular radio-marked hen actually has a brood of young birds, and to determine what that hen and her brood are doing at a particular site. Once disturbed, the birds are no longer useful for observation, so observers must learn to stalk feeding flocks. The biologists' goal is to see the turkeys and classify their flock composition and behavior before the biologists themselves are seen. Those that succeed usually enter the woods with camouflaged clothing, hands, and faces. Radio-tracking antennas are wrapped with camouflaged tape. Even with these precautions, these observers have little hope of extended observation, especially if birds are feeding. Feeding involves

continuous movement of the birds and, therefore, continued reposi-
tioning of the observer. Usually just getting close enough to document
what the birds are doing is a major feat. Drifting through the woods
with them without being detected is virtually impossible.

And this is not only because of the sharp eyes of the turkeys. The
woods are full of creatures that will herald the presence of humans.
Stellar jays do not mince words when they see a human form, and
turkeys recognize the call. Ravens passing overhead will make a gut-
tural comment if an unusual form is seen, and turkeys probably know
a bit of raven language. An unseen deer or elk disturbed by an observer fixated on turkeys will snort or stomp its feet or crash away
through the forest, sure signals to the turkeys that something is amiss.
Red and Abert's squirrels send out alarm notes. The woods are full of
spies; hence there is a feeling of fortuitousness when a radio tracker
manages simply to see a brood, count the turkeys, and determine
whether the birds are feeding or loafing before they silently drift into
the forest.

Rapid departure of spooked birds is not the only behavior that
students of broods may experience. One biologist was moving close
to a brood via radio tracking. Once the birds were seen, she quietly
set aside her receiver and antenna and stalked closer to observe behavior. Unfortunately, her movement was detected by the turkey hen,
who had a very young brood and was extremely protective. Instead
of leading her young away, she signaled them to hide, then charged
the researcher, spreading her wings and hissing loudly. The biologist, already mortified and wanting to minimize disturbance, tried to
move away, but the hen was determined to protect her brood. Wherever the human turned, the turkey moved in front of her, alternating
between hostile behavior and the classic broken-wing act that most
birds use to decoy predators away from nests or young. This went on
for some time, over a large area, before the biologist finally broke
away from the bird and headed back to her vehicle. She had only
gone a short distance when she remembered the radio equipment
she had left at the site and needed to complete her day's work. Returning, she found the irate hen still guarding the area and had to go

through the whole process again before the equipment could be retrieved.

Such behavior on the part of protective hens is not unusual, according to Dr. William Healy, who pioneered studies of imprinted poults on Eastern Wild turkeys in Massachusetts. He notes that turkey hens have been known to drive away broad-winged hawks and red foxes that threatened their broods. One hen was also seen forcing a great horned owl from its perch, and Rio Grande hens in Texas have been seen chasing red-tailed hawks in flight. Interestingly, Healy notes that poults do not hide from snakes but rather circle them at a safe distance while "perting" to alert the brood. Both hens and poults will then mob the reptile until it retires. Larger broods have also been observed mobbing red foxes. More often than not, though young poults dive for cover when an avian or mammalian predator is seen, and they stay crouched and hidden until the hen signals that the coast is clear.

In most cases when a researcher makes a successful approach to a wild brood, behavior observed is either feeding or loafing. During the daylight hours, as far as we know, this is the full repertoire of brood behavior, unless the birds are badly spooked by humans or by natural predators. Hens with broods will move to feeding habitat immediately after leaving the roost and allow their young to spend the morning hours filling their crops. Once fed, they drift into nearby loafing areas and spend a large portion of midday dusting, preening, and snoozing. Good brood habitat consists essentially of suitable roosts and nearby feeding and loafing sites. Cover for escaping from predators is also essential. Each of these habitat components has characteristics of its own.

Roosts for brood flocks differ somewhat from roosts for poultless adults, at least during the first month after hatching. For approximately the first two weeks, chicks cannot fly into a tree, so the hen gathers them under her on the ground. This is a time when losses of hens and poults to predators are undoubtedly high. Poults actually begin short flights at around eight days of age, and they soon learn to hop or fly into lower branches of trees and then move upward to places

of greater safety. For a while, the hen continues to assume a brood-
ing posture on the limb, protecting the entire brood. By the end of a
month, the chicks can flutter into midsized trees and begin to select
branches of their own for sleeping. At six weeks to two months, brood
roosts differ little from the normal summer roosts used by all adult
turkeys.

Locating summer roosts does not require the extreme caution
involved in finding nests or observing broods, but it does have attendant problems. While winter roosts are used over extended periods,
often involve large numbers of birds, and are fairly conspicuous, summer roosts involve small groups of birds, and may be used only once
or twice before flocks move on. In locating winter roosts, an observer
can usually track or follow the birds to the roosting area at sundown,
get a general location based on sound, and return during daylight
hours to confirm the site using the large amounts of droppings, feathers, and tracks that are always present. For summer roosts, the observer must actually see the few birds in the tree, invariably after
dark, then mark the site so that measurements can be made during
daylight. On dark nights, in extensive forests, simply finding the trees
where the birds are sleeping can be difficult. Even more difficult, if
you are not paying attention to your own movements during the
search, is finding your way back to your vehicle in the dark after the
roost has been found. I know of no biologist who has spent the night
lost in the woods, but I know a couple who found their vehicles at
very late hours. If you have not taken good compass readings when
leaving the vehicle, and if you do not pay close attention to your compass on your return, you can get disoriented. Wandering around the
woods in the dark without adequate information on your general location can be an humbling experience. Modern Global Positioning
Satellite (GPS) units should eliminate this problem, as well as allow
biologists to record more accurately the locations of roosts, once
found. Somehow, though, such technology removes some of the challenge and the fun.

Roost tree size and form is similar to those selected in the winter,
but site area is usually smaller. The number of trees per site is usu-

ally less, as would be expected, considering the smaller size and greater dispersal of summer flocks. Birds feeding during the summer may drift over larger areas and may change roost sites more often than in the winter. To some extent, they seem more inclined to sleep where the night finds them. Proximity to food is important.

Feeding sites during early summer are dictated by the special nutritional requirements of young poults. For at least the first six to eight weeks of life, turkey chicks require large amounts of protein to support their rapid body growth. Plants do not provide all of the amino acids needed; invertebrates are essential. Poults must feed themselves from the time they hatch. The hen can guide them to the right places, and perhaps show them food, but they must catch their own bugs. Mom isn't going to bring food to the nest and stick it in their mouths.

Brood feeding habitat is therefore a place with lots of insects or spiders. Bugs are not abundant in the deep forest but are most common in grassy or herbaceous areas, usually meadows. Openings in the forest are therefore critical to broods, and in using these openings, the young birds begin life by walking the fine line between finding enough food and avoiding predators. For a small turkey to move out from the forest canopy is to expose itself to raptors. Small poults are fair game for everything from sharp-shinned hawks to large buteos. They rapidly outgrow their vulnerability to smaller raptors but are potential prey for the larger ones throughout life.

Grass height within openings is important. The grass itself can provide protection for small poults, and density and variety of insects are related to foliage height and density. In general, meadows with dense herbaceous cover at least eight inches tall are required for brood feeding areas. As poults grow larger and less able to hide in low vegetation, dense stands of trees at the edge of meadows become important as escape cover.

What constitutes a suitable sized opening has been somewhat controversial among turkey biologists. At least one worker in Arizona felt strongly that small, well-dispersed openings of perhaps five to ten acres in size were critical for broods. Biologists in other areas felt that the edges of large meadows hundreds of acres in size provided good brood habitat. All agreed that turkeys rarely moved far from the forest edge, and that the centers of large meadows were not used. The fact that arguments occurred suggests that the relation of size and dispersion of forest openings on brood survival could be a lucrative area of research.

Loafing areas, where broods lounge and dust between feeding bouts, are also a somewhat controversial subject among turkey biologists. Workers in Arizona have identified and described fairly definite characteristics that constitute brood loafing sites. Such sites must be near feeding areas, meaning that they will probably be alongside a small forest opening or a meadow. Most loafing sites identified in Arizona were under a dense canopy of mid-sized conifers (eight- to twelve-inch trunk diameters). These sites almost always included a downed snag—dead limbs and the trunk of an old tree that provided the birds with low perches, off the ground. In such a setting, the dark-bodied turkeys are extremely difficult to see, yet they can spot movement in the forest at some distance. They are less vulnerable to predation and can relax more than when feeding in more open habitats. The pine needles and dry leaves surrounding the snags provide good substrate for scratching and dusting. Workers outside of Arizona have questioned the consistent structure of these loafing areas and have found broods resting midday in a variety of settings. The necessity of specific sites for loafing is another area that could use further study.

A clear distinction must be made between loafing cover and escape cover. Loafing sites are chosen and reused; escape cover will be selected spontaneously as a response to danger. Loafing sites are specific and probably constitute a relatively small percentage of an area used by turkeys. Escape cover must be more ubiquitous—on hand to be accessed at a moment's notice. Escape cover, as far as I know, has not been adequately studied. To do so would require intentional flushing of birds, locating the spots they hide, and measuring habitat traits of such spots. If the birds simply leave the area and keep moving, which may well be the case, then escape cover becomes moot as a subject of study.

As the summer progresses, poults grow rapidly, and therefore require different kinds of roosts, food, and cover. By late summer, they are eating more vegetable material and fewer invertebrates. Meadows become less important. By late summer and early fall, a variety of new foods may be available, allowing birds to use a greater diversity of habitats. Mast in the form of acorns and ponderosa pine seeds, piñon nuts, and juniper berries appears. In wetter areas, fruits and berries may be abundant. These foods may constitute the entire turkey diet by late autumn. Fall habitat is therefore composed of increasingly more forest and less meadow. The meadow vegetation is drying up by this time. Insects are less abundant, and turkeys are spending full time seeking seeds and fruits. Concurrent with this, brood flocks begin to assimilate into larger groups and roost sites begin to resemble winter roosts.

In much of Merriam's turkey range, fall food supplies have an extremely spotty distribution. Acorns or pine seeds may be abundant in one area but virtually nonexistent in others. Fruits typically grow in specific and usually limited sites. Yet turkeys seek out these food sources wherever they occur. No one has determined how turkeys adapt to these annual irregularities of food distribution. Do, for example, certain areas more consistently produce acorns than do others? Do older turkeys in flocks remember these areas and return to them? As already noted, evidence from turkey trapping would support this notion. Once a bait station has been maintained in an area during a given winter, turkeys will return to inspect this site during subsequent years. Thus, if a given site produces acorns at least once every three years, chances are a few birds in a flock will remember the site and return to investigate it.

Whatever the case, late summer and fall is probably a critical period for turkeys from a nutritional standpoint. It is the annual period of expected abundance; the time that all wildlife prepares for the difficult months of winter. It is also the period that produces most of the food that will carry over into winter.

In the arid Southwest, such periods of high productivity are not dependable. Both winter precipitation (preparing soils for summer productivity) and summer rainfall (stimulating late summer and fall herbage) vary greatly from year to year. Springs and falls are frequently dry. If winter precipitation is much below normal, the spring drought, with no green food, can be a period of stress. Birds emerge from late winter food deficits and go immediately into reproductive activities. If the previous fall and winter food supply has been limited, the birds will not be physiologically prepared to carry on the frenzy of breeding and the drain of reproduction.

The uncertainties of spring moisture and associated plant growth may be especially important. The high country of the Southwest does not normally warm up early. Snowstorms are common well into April, and freezing temperatures into mid-May. Early spring plant growth is scarce. The birds have no guarantee of a surge of spring foods. This, more than anything else, may explain why turkeys, even Merriam's turkeys, do better in more northerly or easterly regimes where, in spite of severe winters, spring plant growth is relatively dependable. It may also lend credence to the notion that the subspecies is a relative newcomer to the Southwest. Its reproductive cycle seems to be adapted to a different climatic regime, and it performs poorly under normally dry southwestern precipitation patterns. Conversely, dense turkey populations in the Southwest may result only when a series of abnormally wet winters occur.

The long-term differences in relative densities of turkeys across their range seem to support this relationship to moisture. The White Mountains of Arizona and the Chuska Mountains on the Navajo Indian Reservation apparently support higher densities of turkeys than does the western Mogollon Rim or the South Rim of the Grand Canyon. These areas that are further east in the turkey's range have higher fall and winter precipitation and more dependable summer precipitation. An intensive study of turkey productivity across this climatic gradient would be an interesting area of endeavor.

The discussion has led us full circle and back to winter range. We are now ready to discuss what this all means in terms of managing Merriam's turkeys.

15 Roots

As we've seen, our radio-tracking studies disclosed quickly to us that turkey habitat is complex and related to particular behavioral patterns through the turkey year. No major component can be completely missing if the birds are to thrive. No amount of structurally suitable habitat in terms of roosts and cover will suffice if adequate food supplies are not present. An excess of food will not overcome a total lack of roosts and nests secure from predators. Absence of suitable openings for poults to find insects will limit turkey numbers. Lack of ponderosa pine or riparian stringers reaching below the belt of deep winter snows will force the birds to use wintering areas of thick chaparral or dense juniper where they are highly vulnerable to predators.

If we want to create or protect Merriam's turkey habitat, we should therefore emulate southwestern forests. If we want to establish a population of turkeys in a new area, the transplant site should look as much as possible like the habitat of the native population. As already mentioned, our assumption in designing studies was that subspecies are adapted to their native range. We strove to envision the ideal habitat in which Merriam's turkeys had evolved and use this as a model of the bird's requirements.

Whatever the purpose, with increasing human populations and related pressures on western public lands, defining the habitat needs of the southwestern subspecies was becoming increasingly urgent. But even as our new results began to accumulate, I discovered that people in other scientific disciplines viewed the origins, and hence the evolution, of the Merriam's turkey and their habitat differently than we did. A few anthropologists and paleontologists, looking at remains of long-dead birds, had suggested that the southwestern turkey might be a relatively new arrival and could even have been imported from other areas by prehistoric humans. Forest historians have recently suggested that the modern habitat in which we do our studies is much different than the habitat that was present during presettlement times. They feel that Anglos have modified the forest immensely during the past 150 years. And finally, paleobotanists have demonstrated that the habitats that we had come to consider Merriam's turkey native range have not, in fact, existed in the Southwest all that long. Each of these ideas could challenge the presumption that the habitats we assessed in our studies were those to which the bird was originally best adapted.

Vegetation throughout the range of the Merriam's turkey has undoubtedly been modified since Anglo settlement. Two land uses in particular, grazing and timber management (including fire control), have modified the western forests. Virtually no habitats in the Southwest are in the same condition as they were when Europeans arrived.

Much of the southwestern ponderosa pine forest was once much more open with widely spaced large trees. Ecologists of Northern Arizona University suggest that heavy livestock grazing and fire suppression have combined to increase tree density, in places as much as fortyfold, while decreasing production of herbaceous and shrub vegetation. However, these same forest ecologists emphatically warn against oversimplified application of their findings and note that prior to settlement of the Southwest, extreme variation within limited areas and across full regions existed. Observations of early naturalists and foresters confirm such early diversity. Descriptions varied depending on time and place. In 1875, J. T. Rothrock, traveling with the Wheeler party in the Zuni Mountains, noted dense forests of pine and fir. In the same area, he described a fine open parklike region, with a large growth of yellow pine and fir covering the hillsides. Wheeler himself described Arizona's White Mountains as a densely timbered range. He also referred to dense timber growth with fertile valleys and open glades near the San Francisco Mountains. Edgar A. Mearns wrote in 1890 of the San Francisco Mountains and Mogollon

Range as wooded and adorned with many beautiful parks and elevated valleys. In 1904, a forester remarked on the exceptionally heavy stands of young timber along the Mogollon Rim, and in 1911, another forester noted that the ponderosa pine forest was made up of blackjack, with an occasional mature yellow pine fast declining in vigor.

Other elements of Merriam's turkey habitat have changed as well over the past 150 years. The birds consistently move to lower elevations in the winter, using portions of the piñon-juniper and deciduous riparian vegetation types for winter range. Tree densities in the piñon-juniper woodlands have increased throughout the range of the Merriam's turkey, and in many places, stringers of ponderosa pine extending downward into the woodlands have been logged or burned. Such pine stringers once provided winter roosting areas that allowed turkeys to exploit winter food resources, such as piñon nuts, juniper berries, and grass seed heads, that were less likely to be buried by snow at the lower elevations.

Similarly, stands of large cottonwoods along streams, such as lower Oak Creek near Sedona and the lower San Pedro River near Kearny, once harbored wintering turkey populations and allowed them to feed into the upper edge of grassland and desert habitats. Along most of the streams of the Southwest, grazing and settlement have disrupted use of these riparian stands by turkeys. Also, the turkey populations using these riparian stands, because they were more accessible than many other wintering populations, were among the first to be extirpated by early, unregulated hunting. The flock memory that led birds to return to these low elevation habitats may have simply been eliminated, leaving only groups of birds that wintered elsewhere.

However we view it, current habitat is not the same as that which existed before humans arrived. The structure of forests and woodlands have changed, and some components have been greatly reduced or have disappeared. In the case of the pine stringers and riparian forests, a century or more would be required to replace them, if replacement were possible. So, when we assess current habitat, we must keep in mind that this is not necessarily the habitat that existed 150 years ago. Merriam's turkeys may not necessarily be well adapted to it and may instead be perpetually stressed survivors.

And some have suggested that the ancestors of these survivors did not evolve in the Southwest to begin with. Lyndon Hargrave, the same young scientist who studied Merriam's turkeys in 1939, was apparently the first scientist to suggest that early Indians might have imported Merriam's turkey. After his brief career as a wildlife biologist, Hargrave became an archeologist for the Museum of Northern Arizona, but his interest in birds remained. He apparently formed his hypothesis regarding Merriam's turkey origins while working on the Navajo Reservation during the 1940s, but the Navajos had a story that predated Hargrave. In 1940, F. J. Newcomb, a trader on the Navajo Reservation, wrote that tribal legends held that the wild turkey found in the mountainous sections of the Navajo country were probably descendants of turkeys raised by the Pueblo people who once occupied the area. Hargrave was wandering the Navajo reservation about the same time as Newcomb, and he may well have heard the same story. He may, on the other hand, have developed the theory from his own observations of turkey remains in Anasazi ruins.

Whatever the case, other scientists have taken this idea further. Charmion McKusick, a private archaeologist living in Globe, Arizona, has measured hundreds of turkey bones from Indian ruins in the southwestern United States and northern Mexico. She hypothesizes that Merriam's turkeys originated from a particular strain of domestic birds that had been introduced into Mesa Verde, Canyon de Chelly, and other locations by the Anasazi culture about A.D. 500 and later escaped into the wild, as this early Pueblo culture declined. As noted earlier, McKusick suggested that the Merriam's turkey is more closely related anatomically to the eastern subspecies than to Mexican birds and, therefore, might have been brought in by way of eastern trade routes.

Not all archeologists accept this concept of prehistoric feral origins for Merriam's turkeys. Immanuel Breitburg, using measurements of turkey leg and wing bones, suggested that the Merriam's turkey was present in its historic range before the Anasazi, Sinagua, and

Mogollon cultures and that the Anasazi domesticated them fifteen hundred to two thousand years ago. Breitburg supports McKusick in suggesting that the Merriam's turkey is closely related to eastern races, but makes no judgment regarding its relationship with other subspecies.

As we've seen, Karen Mock's recent work on turkey DNA supports McKusick and Breitburg in placing the Merriam's turkey genetically close to the eastern subspecies and more distant from the Gould's turkey, even though it superficially looks more like the Gould's. Unfortunately, her work does not yet answer clearly how the subspecies expanded its range into the Southwest. She and geneticists at Washington State University are planning to analyze DNA in tissue from mummified turkeys found in Anasazi ruins, and their findings may shed light here.

Paleontologists Amadeo Rea and David Steadman both suggest that fossil records, or lack of them, suggest feral origins for Merriam's turkey. They point out that no fossil remains of *Meleagris gallopavo* predating the Anasazi have been found in Arizona, Colorado, or New Mexico. A few remains of an extinct turkey, *Meleagris crassipes,* have been found as far north as the Grand Canyon and as far south as Nuevo Leon in Mexico. This bird was present until well after prehistoric humans arrived some twelve thousand years ago. The cause of its extinction can only be guessed. Most likely, its habitat simply disappeared as a result of postglacial climatic change at the end of the Pleistocene. However the Merriam's turkey arrived, no evidence yet exists revealing its presence in Arizona, New Mexico, or Colorado earlier than about twenty-five hundred years ago.

Paleobotany of the Southwest indirectly supports the idea that Merriam's turkeys are relative newcomers, although it provides a wider potential period of arrival. Studies of vegetation remains in fossil packrat middens and studies of pollen layers in natural lakes both indicate that forest species normally associated with Merriam's turkey were virtually absent from Arizona, New Mexico, and Colorado ten thousand years ago. Before that, southwestern highlands were covered mainly with spruce and fir, species now more typical of higher elevations in the Rocky Mountains or of boreal forests in Canada. Such forests would today represent the extreme upper altitudinal or latitudinal limits of summer range for turkeys. They probably lack the seed-producing species, such as oaks, piñon pine, or ponderosa pine, required for fall and winter foods. Winter snow depths would be too great for turkeys to survive. The area was apparently better suited to blue grouse. Ponderosa pine wasn't well established throughout most of the Merriam's turkey range until about eight thousand years ago, and the forest distribution in the Southwest as we know it did not stabilize until some twenty-six hundred years ago.

What we call Merriam's turkeys therefore probably could not have been present in the Southwest until at least eight thousand years ago, and they may have arrived much more recently than that. This possible late arrival, seemingly associated with the Anasazi, does not necessarily support the hypothesis that humans imported the birds. Sporadic movements of thirty to forty airline miles over a week's time are not unusual for modern Merriam's turkeys; hence they are entirely capable of expanding their range over large areas. It seems likely that suitable corridors for turkey movements existed along rivers that extend into the Southwest from either Mexico or from eastern habitats across the Great Plains.

Meleagris gallopavo occurred as far north as the current U.S.-Mexico border during the Pleistocene. These populations would therefore seem to be a potential source for turkeys expanding naturally as southwestern pine forests expanded. The potential for prehistoric immigration of turkeys from eastern forests into the southern Rocky Mountains is difficult to assess. The paleobotany of the Great Plains to the east of Merriam's turkey range suggests that spruce and aspen forests covered the northern Great Plains until some twelve thousand years ago. Warming climate augmented by fire converted the northern plains from boreal forests to grasslands. The southern Plains were apparently prairie, with some intrusions of woodland and forest, including ponderosa pine. Little is known about the history of the vegetation of the various rivers across the plains. Cottonwood, oak, sycamore, and willow could have sporadically provided corridors for turkeys to move to the Southwest from easterly ranges.

J. Stokely Ligon, in his 1946 book on the Merriam's turkey, suggested that such contact occurred along the Arkansas, South Platte, or Canadian Rivers. At the time he wrote, he felt that these connecting threads of turkey habitat had long been severed, leaving the Merriam's free of contact with the Eastern or low-altitude strains. He stated that the accounts of Thomas Say and James W. Abert indicated that the range of the turkey in the mid-1880s extended without a break from Oklahoma up the Arkansas and Purgatory Rivers to Raton Pass, and connected with populations down the Canadian River to Oklahoma. However, I've found nothing in the diaries of these or other explorers to suggest that suitable turkey habitat extended from the plains along the South Platte or Arkansas Rivers during historic times. Virtually all the early expeditions following the Arkansas westward first remark upon western turkeys at approximately the mouth of the Purgatory River.

Records of turkeys along the Canadian River are mixed. In 1823, Edwin James, heading eastward along the Canadian with the Stephen Long expedition, noted the first encounter of turkeys after leaving the Rocky Mountains at a point near the present Texas/Oklahoma border. Neither Zebulon Pike (1809) nor Amiel Weeks Whipple (1858) recorded turkeys on the Canadian across the Texas panhandle, but Abert, in his 1845 trip eastward, mentioned turkeys at several sites between the present New Mexico–Texas line and the Oklahoma border.

I have as yet found no journals that specifically describe presettlement habitats or wildlife populations along the North Canadian or Cimarron Rivers. While both of these rivers arise near the easternmost extension of known Merriam's turkey range, they, too, were apparently devoid of continuous forest vegetation across the high plains. Randolph Marcy (1852) found scattered turkey populations up the Red River to approximately the center of the Texas Panhandle, but no further. Richard Dodge, in *Plains of the Great West* (1876), described the rivers across Kansas and the Oklahoma panhandle as having low banks and wide, shallow beds filled with sand. The bottomlands were very broad, without trees or shrubbery, except for occasional small growths of willow, scarcely larger than switches. This is not a picture of habitat for a forest-dwelling bird.

Thus, based on Abert's 1845 journal, the Canadian River is the best candidate for a historic riparian connector between eastern turkey subspecies and Merriam's turkey historic range, and such a connector may have occurred only sporadically. Nonetheless, I suspect the opportunity occasionally occurred during the past twenty-five hundred years for turkeys to expand along this river from Texas and Oklahoma into New Mexico.

A human factor is therefore not essential to explain turkey presence in the Southwest. For that matter, we actually have no reason to assume a single origin for southwestern birds. The birds of southeastern Colorado and northeastern New Mexico, for example, may have originated through native expansion of birds up the Canadian River. They could be from Rio Grande or eastern turkey stock, or both. The turkeys of the Sacramento Mountains and Guadalupe Mountains may have been derived from turkeys expanding up the Pecos or Rio Grande Rivers and may have had Rio Grande turkey ancestors. The turkeys of southwestern New Mexico and southern Arizona could have come from the San Pedro and Santa Cruz Rivers, thereby originating in Gould's turkey habitat. And, who knows? The early Indians might have moved a few turkeys around as well. Certainly modern biologists have and, unfortunately, these transplants have so fully mixed with wild populations that even the powerful tools of molecular genetics may not untangle the bird's origins. For now, our best hope may lie in the stories to be told by genes of birds preserved by the Anasazi, fifteen centuries ago.

16 Of Turkeys and Biologists

By about 1989, the new Merriam's turkey study was up and running. The methodology was established, and we were fortunate in having good assistants on the ground. Cheryl Mollohan and Brian Wakeling, both with fresh master's degrees, were handling all of the fieldwork. Much of the project logistics was being handled out of the Phoenix office. In truth, I found myself feeling rather unnecessary and was spending much time at home, writing up old information. The Chevelon study area was a four-hour drive from my home in Chino Valley, so work trips to the area usually involved weeklong stays. I realized that I truly preferred to be at home. Also, I realized that once the project planning had been done and the crews adequately trained in the necessary techniques, my work was pretty much over, at least until the final reports were required. And the new assistants were entirely capable of writing those reports.

It would seem that, after the prolonged effort in getting a decent habitat study up and running, I would want to hang around for the results. I spent a year trying to convince myself of the fact, but the simple truth was that I no longer wanted to work for the agency. Too much had changed. I found myself regularly traveling to group meetings designed to discuss laboriously the kind of decisions that I had always made on my own. I had enough years accumulated to draw a decent retirement, I didn't particularly care for my supervisors, and I was constantly objecting to ideas they brought up. Too often I heard myself angrily saying, "We tried that twenty years ago." Worse yet, I could see they weren't listening. I felt disempowered, I guess.

One day, in one of these meetings, which happened to be at

Chevelon, the discussion turned to the possibility of a study of fall turkey hunting to see if we should go back to the lottery system in licensing hunters. The idea, in spite of my protestations, was getting strong support. It seemed that we had turned the clock back twenty years. As I sat and listened, I realized that I had simply been around too long. I was becoming an obstructionist in the minds of the people in the room. By staying in the field so long, I had finally ended up in the classic situation wherein all of my supervisors, even at the very top level of the department, were younger and less experienced than I was. They had no sense of departmental history, and I was having major difficulties showing respect for their ideas or opinions. I felt myself become distant from the discussion at the table, and I left as soon as my presence was no longer required, with a strong sense of relief, knowing that I had made a necessary decision. Someone else would design any new studies that might come along. It took me almost a year to wrap up reports and hand the project off to Brian Wakeling, and I retired the first of April in 1990.

But my involvement with turkeys didn't end with retirement. Between 1988 and 1992, bridging the time of my departure from the Arizona Game and Fish Department, I worked with a group of wild turkey specialists to develop guidelines for managing Merriam's wild turkeys. We addressed all aspects of turkey management—including census, hunt regulation, and predator control—but we focused much of our effort on habitat. During this series of meetings with fellow biologists, I observed how quickly we reached the limits of our knowledge. I also noticed that our individual studies, based on scientific method, did not necessarily bring us to easy consensus on many details regarding turkey habitat needs. Our varied experiences often led instead to rather animated debate followed by laboriously forged compromise. The process was fascinating, and the product, I believe, excellent. It produced, at least for the time, the best directives available for management of turkeys in the western United States. But it also left those involved humbled by the magnitude of our differences and seeking new ways to refine our research.

I was surprised to discover that conflicts over the guidelines did not end within our committee. After we had forged our viewpoints into a manuscript that we all endorsed, we ran head-on into wildlife managers from several western states, who informed us that the guidelines could not be used in the format we had produced. I don't think any of us ever understood quite why. Staff members of the National Wild Turkey Federation then agreed to draft a more practical document, using our information. Their revision, when finished, was rejected by our committee. We felt it rendered our recommendations ineffective. After prolonged discourse, we refused to accept the Turkey Federation's draft, and the Turkey Federation refused to publish the committee's version. The Colorado Division of Wildlife ultimately printed the committee's guidelines, unendorsed by the National Wild Turkey Federation.

This event, more than any other in my career, motivated me to write this book. I exited the guidelines development process amazed that so much dissension had occurred amidst a group of scientists who had so much presumably objective information on a single subspecies of turkey. I could see that the early differences between the biologists within the committee had been caused to some extent by geography. These specialists came from Arizona, New Mexico, Colorado, Wyoming, and South Dakota, and their concerns over sensitivity of the turkey to changing habitat varied with locality. Interestingly, the biologists from states within the historic range of the Merriam's turkey seemed to be the most cautious regarding the effects of human activities on turkey habitat quality. They worried especially about the losses of large ponderosa pine trees used as roosts, small meadows for brood habitat, and specific sites within the forest for loafing and dusting. Biologists from Wyoming and South Dakota, where turkeys had been established by transplants during the past fifty years, seemed less concerned about forest modifications. On the whole, their observations led them to believe that Merriam's turkeys could live with smaller roost trees, larger meadows, and a wide array of forested sites for loafing areas if, indeed, such areas were even needed. No one seemed overly worried about nesting sites, an element of habitat that one would intuitively assume to be a bottleneck in turkey productivity.

Resistance to the guidelines from the state turkey managers was harder for me to explain. Geography was, I believe, again a part of the problem, albeit for different reasons. Perhaps no single set of guidelines could ever address turkey management in every state. Certainly no single set of guidelines could address the array of politics affecting wildlife management over such a large area, perhaps running counter to agendas of some local wildlife managers, hunters, loggers, ranchers, and environmentalists. If the guidelines had satisfied everyone, they probably would have been useless.

Whatever the case, the management biologists claimed that the guidelines could not be used in the form in which they were written. But even as these claims were being made, I was using the guidelines to assess turkey habitat in southern Utah under a contract with the U.S. Forest Service. I had a crew of field biologists who, with a few days of training in the use of the guidelines, were quite capable of evaluating large expanses of turkey habitat on the Dixie National Forest.

Conflicts with the Turkey Federation were our greatest surprise, because the Federation had sponsored our effort to begin with. Our differences with them stemmed in part, I believe, from our respective perceptions of the intended audience. The Wild Turkey Federation staff, housed in the southeastern United States where public lands are scarce, seemed to see the document as a treatise for turkey hunters and private landowners involved in turkey transplant and habitat improvement programs. Such activities have been extremely successful in the eastern United States, where much of the turkey habitat occurs on private forests that have repeatedly regrown after many cycles of logging. Eastern turkey biologists have a certain faith that they can work with landowners to recreate habitat and to restore turkey populations where they have ceased to exist. In the moist eastern forests, they may accomplish this in a relatively short time.

However, the western biologists writing the guidelines saw their audience as state and federal resource specialists in charge of timber, grazing, and recreation management on public lands. They specifically addressed logging and grazing practices on National Forests, which encompass a large proportion of the Merriam's turkey range. Western forests are dry and fragile. They do not regenerate quickly. We cannot yet predict the long-term effects of traditional land uses, especially logging and grazing, on the habitat of wild species, and we are not confident that we can restore habitat. We worry that current land uses may permanently modify our forests. Until we know more, we are necessarily protective of existing conditions.

In attempting to influence land management practices on western lands we seldom deal directly with private commercial users. We seek instead to influence biologists, silviculturists, or range specialists within land management agencies as they design logging or grazing programs. To be an effective part of the process, western wildlife biologists must clearly promote specific habitat conditions in the technical language of the timber and range managers.

Over the past decade, since the Merriam's turkey guidelines were completed and published, I've reflected at length over the complexities we encountered in implementing knowledge of a single turkey subspecies. I've come to realize that writing the guidelines was only a beginning. Everyone involved in the guidelines committee was within the wildlife profession, and all had the common goal of helping Merriam's turkeys. Yet the guidelines were published only after many months of dissension and ultimately in the face of unresolved conflict.

Decades of field research in several states had preceded the development of the guidelines, and complex decisions had been involved in the initiation of each research project. Every project required time, perhaps years, to develop essential technology and expertise before accumulation of useful data began. Once up and running, virtually no adequate field study could be completed in less than five years. The process had therefore been long and tedious before our committee convened.

Implementation of the guidelines by the various agencies that accepted them has only begun. They will be adapted and modified to suit the needs of local wildlife agency administrators and biologists. And, of course, this single set of guidelines will run counter to the demands of commercial interests, as well as the goals of biologists managing a myriad of other wildlife species.

In the midst of all of this, turkey research continues. Old knowledge is reviewed for its accuracy and new knowledge accumulates. Guidelines such as the ones we developed begin to be obsolete the moment they are published. They will be tested and modified. Some recommendations will be rejected, and at some future time, new guidelines will be written. Confusion and dissension will occur again within the turkey management ranks. At this point, I have begun to wonder if scientific management of wildlife might be a myth. I wonder even more if the lay public, isolated from the process, unaware of its complexity, and increasingly threatened by its economic ramifications, will continue to support the wildlife profession.

17 Good Housekeeping

As our efforts to develop management guidelines demonstrated, knowing turkey habitat requirements is only the beginning of the problem faced by wildlife managers. Application of this knowledge may lead to conflicts with logging or grazing; with summer home developments and recreational uses; and with the habitat needs of other wildlife species. The most difficult part of the wildlife biologist's job is blending these potentially conflicting land uses.

The initial effect of any timber-cutting program on turkeys will be to modify the structural habitat—the shape of the woods. Logging can range from light selective cutting, where only a few trees are taken from scattered sites in the forest, to extensive clear-cutting, where large acreages are denuded of trees and the land stands temporarily bare. Many possibilities exist between these extremes—more intensive selective cuts, where more trees are taken from each site; age-class cuts, which take all trees greater than a certain size and leave smaller ones for replacement; shelter wood cuts, which leave a few large trees to provide shade for the regrowth of species intolerant to sun; and seed-tree cuts, which leave a few larger trees to disperse seeds and regenerate the forest. From a forester's standpoint, each of these have a purpose, and the type of cut made will be influenced by economic considerations and by the biological nature of the tree species being harvested.

From the standpoint of turkey habitat, the names of these forms of timber harvest mean little. What counts is the shape of the woods after the harvest is complete and, in fact, different types of cuts can produce similar shapes. Properly done, logging can be beneficial to turkeys. Small openings in the forest can be produced by selective cutting or by small clear-cuts. Seed tree and shelter-wood cuts both initially yield open stands, leaving large, scattered trees. Only subsequent treatment will determine the actual management strategy being used. The biologist must be able to envision the type of forest needed to provide optimum habitat. He and the forester must then cooperate to create or protect the forest forms required for turkeys, as well as a host of other wildlife species, while allocating timber desired by loggers.

Coordinating logging and wildlife habitat management is therefore a complicated, but possible, process. It is further complicated by other land uses. The effects of grazing on turkey numbers are not well understood. Potentially, ruminants compete with turkeys for food at all seasons of the year. Cattle, sheep, or elk on summer range can alter meadows to the point that they will be useless for broods. Heavy grazing of grasses on winter range eliminates seed heads that may be the only available source of late winter food during years of poor mast production. And ruminants will also compete with turkeys for mast. Experimental evaluation of grazing effects on turkeys is badly needed.

In Arizona and over much of the Southwest, logging is presently in abeyance. Pressure from environmental groups has taken much of the blame for the decline of the logging industry but, in truth, heavy cutting over the past fifty years has decreased the supply of timber-sized trees in southwestern ponderosa pine forests to the point that logging is not economically viable. This is probably a temporary situation. As the present young forests mature, timber companies will again be seeking trees. When this happens, biologists will once again be called upon to participate in timber sale design. With the new information gained, they should be better prepared than they have been in the past.

Spring grazing of meadows by livestock or large numbers of elk can reduce the quality of meadows needed by turkey poults seeking insects. Grazing can also alter the fire regime of a forest. Removal of herbaceous plants can reduce the fuels required to carry low-level fires that kill tree seedlings and promote a more open, grassy under-story. Heavy summer grazing by sheep and cattle during the late 1800s and early 1900s is now recognized as a major factor in reducing fire frequency, and thereby creating the dense stands of young ponde-rosa pine that occurred late in the twentieth century over much of the southwestern forests.

Finally, summer homes built in forest meadows can eliminate habitat for turkey broods. Historically, early homesteaders and ranch-ers claimed the meadows for their farms or ranch headquarters. These openings became the only private deeded lands within many of the national forests. Most of these areas succeeded poorly as farms and few of them now hold active ranch houses. As ranching has declined, these meadows have been subdivided for summer homes or, at times, permanent residences.

So other land uses can affect turkey habitat. Further complicat-ing habitat management is the fact that clear visions of the habitat desired are difficult to form. If turkeys were the only species of con-cern, biologists could gradually modify existing habitats, all the while monitoring turkey response, until some optimum condition was at-tained. This would not necessarily satisfy the needs of loggers or ranchers, or of other wildlife species.

So what standard do we use in managing the forest? Do we simply leave it alone on the assumption that, over time, it will evolve into the best of all forest worlds? With the demands on forest resources cre-ated by current human densities, I doubt that such nonintervention is possible. Or do we manage for some theoretical maximum diver-sity, on the assumption that all needs will be at least partially satisfied? Intuitively, I suspect that maximum diversity alone is not a reliable guide. It would almost certainly result in a highly broken and ma-nipulated forest. Do we manage toward some hypothetical historic condition, representing a time when human, or at least European, effects were nonexistent? If so, what were these historic conditions? And, returning to our original, single-minded concern, were such his-toric conditions always the best possible habitat for Merriam's turkeys?

And what is the truth about historic conditions? I believe that we often give undue credence to "old" information, when the same stories, told today, might arouse disbelief. Historic records, even if accurate, represent only snapshots in time, catching isolated circumstances. With a species such as the turkey, inclined to boom and bust dynamics, impressions formed by observers are influenced by the year, location, or season the observations were made. Writers are traditionally more likely to record exceptional conditions than the norm. Large numbers of birds apparently occurred now and then, but we do not know if numbers were consistently greater than they are now, or if observers were merely recording peaks. We still periodically still see years of extraordinary turkey abundance. Wildlife has traditionally been the source of tall tales. The same folks who comfortably accept such stories regarding historical turkey numbers may demand statistically reliable surveys and 95 percent confidence levels from modern turkey biologists making annual hunt recommendations.

Southwestern wildlife populations were poorly documented between 1865 and 1940, when turkeys apparently declined throughout the Southwest. Heavy logging and unrestrained grazing by livestock certainly modified habitats. Scattered homesteaders living off the land pursued wildlife year-round. By 1940, Merriam's turkeys had been extirpated over much of their historic range within conifer forests. All wild turkeys were gone from most of the cottonwood bottoms of the Rio Grande, Gila, San Pedro, and Santa Cruz Rivers.

The relative importance of hunting versus habitat change in these turkey population declines is difficult to assess. Forest historians currently suggest that the presettlement forest in the Southwest was an open, parklike stand of mature ponderosa pine, with a lush, grassy understory. But the record isn't clear, and if such a forest was present, it may not all have been used by turkeys. Once more, we hasten to conceptualize prehistoric conditions using limited information, but demand scientific rigor in the form of radio-tracking data in assessing modern habitat requirements. As we learn more about the long-term changes in habitats—resulting from climatic change, natural disasters, and human activity (including that of Anasazi, Sinagua, Hopi, Navajo, Apache, Yavapai, Hualapai, Spanish, and Anglos)—we must

acknowledge that reaching for some ideal of historic, essentialist perfection is probably unrealistic. We can design a habitat, but it must be
based on the best current knowledge, and it must clearly be acknowledged as our own product.

Such management of landscapes to benefit wildlife is a relatively
new endeavor. For the greater part of this century, wildlife was viewed
as a by-product of other land uses. If logging created more food for
white-tailed deer, this was good, and it helped to justify logging. If
ranchers made watering holes for cattle, and turkeys, deer, or ante-
lope used these, this too was good, and it gave the rancher an added
sense of accomplishment. Wildlife managers of the 1940s, 1950s, and
1960s believed that all of these land uses were compatible. Some of
us still do, but we know the emphasis must change. We know we
must still live from products of the land, but the capabilities of the
land must be our first consideration, not the economic bottom line.

18 Counting Coop

During the past twenty-five years, due largely to the abundance of data gathered through radio-tracking studies, we have learned much about the role of various habitat elements for wild turkeys. We are only beginning, however, to assess existing landscapes and to identify limited or missing habitat components as they relate to the welfare of the bird. And we have hardly begun at all to monitor effects of habitat change on bird or mammal populations. After a half-century of turkey research and management, we still do not have simple or economically feasible methods for accurately monitoring changes in turkey population size as they relate to various habitat manipulations or hunting strategies.

Population changes in some wildlife species may be insidious, occurring slowly over long periods. Turnover in wildlife agency personnel is such that few individuals now remain long in any given place. And wildlife agencies themselves are usually poor archivists. Determining the history of land use for a particular area is often difficult. Determining past land management strategies can be impossible. As a result, no historical perspective develops, and gradual degradation of habitat, and hence declines in wild populations, may occur without being detected by relatively insensitive monitoring methods. This is accentuated by the fact that, where field surveys are carried out, succeeding generations of managers may modify survey techniques, thereby hampering long-term comparisons of population information. The value of surveys is destroyed by abrupt changes in methodology without calibration to past techniques, or cessation of surveys for extended periods.

Our lack of good turkey census methods is not due to lack of effort. One of the first projects carried out by the research branch of the Arizona Game and Fish Department was an evaluation of the roadside survey. Ron Smith, newly hired as a biometrician for the department, established ten routes in the White Mountains in 1958, and research personnel ran these routes annually through 1961. The study concluded that such surveys would require an impractical level of effort to detect turkey population trends within each turkey management unit. In 1969, I looked at three years of roadside survey data from the Moqui study and compared them with the earlier White Mountain data. The results of this evaluation once again suggested that, while the method would detect change in population trends and composition, the amount of effort required was more than could be devoted to a single species by management personnel. As a result of these evaluations, wildlife managers quit making formal turkey surveys on established routes and substituted opportunistic counts and classification of turkeys seen during routine patrol of their units. This eliminated hope of detecting trends in turkey numbers in a statistically reliable manner.

In 1985 and 1986, Heather Green, a graduate student at Northern Arizona University, relocated all of the White Mountain routes and, with the help of Arizona Game and Fish Department personnel, repeated them once more. Her results suggested that the turkey numbers had declined by 76 percent over the twenty-five years since 1961, while the number of turkeys killed by hunters had increased by 83 percent between the 1960s period and the 1980s period. Unfortunately, the Moqui survey routes could not be repeated to see if a similar decline in turkey numbers had occurred in that area. Thus, it seems that, while monitoring turkey numbers accurately on a year-to-year basis throughout the turkey range is not possible with available personnel and funds, periodic intensive surveys in selected areas can detect important changes.

Also, while we can measure habitat use in limited areas using radio-tracking studies, we are only beginning to blend the findings of these local studies with more expansive habitat monitoring and evaluation now being carried out via satellite imagery and aerial photography. We cannot yet predict what large-scale habitat changes mean in terms of wild turkey numbers. Habitat monitoring is a relatively new discipline which, in a sense, reverses the process we used in studying turkeys. Whereas in research we watched turkeys to identify their preferred habitat, then measured it; in monitoring, we measure the habitat and decide if it is suitable for turkeys. Theoretically, if something is missing, we should be able to manage the forest to increase the missing element. But if we manage habitats this intensively, I believe we are then obligated to continue to monitor the effects of our actions. Too often, in the past, we have created change but failed to observe the consequences.

The measurement of habitat characteristics is a complex process, and the interpretation and application of the results are even more difficult. Reasons for assessing turkey habitat are varied. They may include evaluating areas prior to logging, grazing, mining, or prescribed burns. A corollary to this would be predicting the effects of any land use on turkeys and incorporating the needs of the birds into the plan of use. A second purpose might be evaluating an area in preparation for habitat improvement and recommending vegetation modifications that would make it more suitable for turkeys. In many cases, these two purposes could be combined: building turkey habitat improvement into a logging or grazing plan for a national forest. A third reason might be evaluating the suitability of an area for receiving turkey transplants. A final reason, and the most difficult, would be periodically monitoring unpredicted changes in habitat that might affect turkey numbers. Such unfocused monitoring is expensive and difficult to justify in the face of more pressing wildlife management needs. For any of these, the evaluation process will have the same goal—to identify habitat elements that may be missing or in limited supply.

I believe that good monitoring is more important for Merriam's turkey habitats than it may be for eastern turkey subspecies. This western subspecies requires large areas of habitat to survive. It exists in a dry and relatively fragile environment that recovers slowly from any modifications. Changes, via burning or logging, that will last for centuries can happen in a few days. In the arid Southwest, we cannot restore habitat as rapidly as can be done in eastern forests.

Thus, while we have gathered large amounts of information regarding Merriam's turkey habitat needs, we have not developed ways to implement this information into turkey management processes. The uneasy rejection of our management guidelines by western states' turkey managers is symptomatic of this problem. We perhaps know more than wildlife managers can conveniently apply on the ground. In virtually all western states, turkey populations are monitored through minimal field surveys, usually roadside counts or spring gobbling counts, methods that are known to have poor precision. These may be supplemented by harvest data gathered through mail questionnaires to licensed hunters. These techniques suffice as long as turkey populations remain secure and stable; they are unlikely to detect an impending crisis.

This situation is not likely to change quickly, for turkeys or other wildlife, simply because the funds and manpower do not exist to increase sampling intensity or to implement improved survey methodology where it exists. Some states are now beginning to use hunters and other nonbiologists to assist in survey programs. Such involvement of laymen in monitoring has the twofold benefit of increasing available manpower and making the public a part of the management process.

This latter benefit is important. I believe that the development of "professionalism" in wildlife agencies has resulted in reduced field effort due to limited trained personnel and an attitude of authoritarianism among biologists. We are now caught in the dilemma of not accepting field data gathered by anyone except paid agency employees and, at the same time, not being able to afford enough professionals to do the job. As a result, much work goes undone. In the meantime, much of turkey management is based on harvest data— all of which is provided by hunters. We need badly to involve the hobby naturalist and naturalist hunter in our monitoring efforts.

19 Blind Faith

This has been a rather lengthy essay on a single subspecies—an effort to define it on a more visceral level. Perhaps the primary conclusion to be drawn from the effort is that we can never know another creature as well as we know ourselves, and our inability as a species to overcome our own overpopulation and warlike tendencies remind us that we're not long on self-knowledge.

We can't describe or define a subspecies in a few short words—they do not live within a habitat; the habitat is a part of the definition of the creature. In spite of the wild turkey's uniqueness as a native bird, it is nonetheless valued more as a huntable game species and less as an unusual element in the ecosystem. Its value as a game species has been its salvation, and hunters alone have seen to its security and restoration. Domestication has made turkeys so common that the species is taken for granted by the larger, nonhunting public, yet the wild bird's continued existence, its very ability to adapt and survive, makes it a subject worth study. During the eighteenth and nineteenth centuries, when other large, ground-dwelling birds such as the dodo and or the greater auk were extirpated, the turkey survived. With help from hunters, it has now irrupted to new numerical heights in many parts of North America. Probably no other wild species has become so completely representative of North America or provides a better example of success of modern wildlife management.

The wild turkey of the west—the Merriam's turkey—remains a conundrum. Its origins are vague; its preferred habitat still somewhat of a mystery. But it should be apparent by now that the phenomenon of "habitat" is not simple. The complex that constitutes Merriam's turkey habitat is associated with a mosaic of behaviors designed to avoid predators, survive severe climate, and stave off malnutrition. While we, as biologists, understand habitat on a conceptual level and have learned much about the seasonal behavior or nutritional needs of the birds, we still struggle to apply this knowledge. Our increasing understanding of habitat complexity has, if anything, reduced our confidence in manipulating forests. Yet we must participate in programs that affect forest habitats. This is imposed by nature, in the form of wildfire, drought, and other vagaries of weather; by loggers and ranchers, who have traditionally had the greatest and most visible effects on turkey habitat; and by encroaching rural dwellers who, in their desire to return to nature, are using it up.

Only during the past thirty years, as a result of efforts by Fred Phillips and others, have wildlife biologists been given any say in planning the use of forest lands. In the past, ranching and logging drove management decisions. Wildlife essentially took whatever was left. The increased urbanization of the West, increased concern over wildlife, and reduced political clout of loggers and ranchers have perhaps given wildlife a new and larger constituency. This is a benevolent side effect of economic growth in the western states that is inevitably temporary. The same forces that may have reduced the hold of ranching and logging on public lands are now turning vast landscapes of the West into small ranches, housing developments, and shopping malls. In the long run, this is a much more permanent form of habitat destruction.

Traditional rural dwellers—loggers, ranchers, and farmers—viewed wildlife as a fringe benefit of their lifestyle. They modified habitats and manipulated predator populations with a sort of numb complacency regarding long-term effects. Loss of a species, especially a nuisance species or predator, was of little concern and quite often a goal to be attained. They pushed the wildland toward domesticity and considered wildlife, land, trees, and grass theirs to exploit. They took pride in their ability to survive and live on the land, and in their skills in exploiting wildland resources.

Modern rural dwellers are a different breed. Few of them make their living from the land, but they take a certain pride in country living. To live away from the city and survive on the land is the ultimate attainment for those who espouse the rural lifestyle. Association with wildlife is a part of this image. But as the wildlands are subdivided; the dangerous, competitive, or nuisance species destroyed; and rural domesticity attained, the image becomes a myth, and the overgrown country boy who flaunts it is only an actor, imitating his ancestors. Yet, with his five-acre ranch, his cowboy hat or roper cap, his four-wheel drive pickup, his snuff can, and his rifle in the window rack, he plays out a role on a real and vulnerable landscape, which his actions continue to modify.

At the other extreme is the urbanite living in an atmosphere of rapid events and instant gratification. Where the logger or rancher may set a series of events into play that result in a single crop each year, or perhaps a single crop decades in the future, mechanized city life encourages instant results. You push a button on your remote and observe the life story of a wild species, canned especially for television and interpreted for you by a deep male voice that, by its very tone, usually predicts devastation and doom. Yet more often than not, the narrator is just another urban dweller reading from a script produced by a series of urban dwellers who may or may not have sought the advice of someone with knowledge of the species. And the story the narrator tells about wildlife is necessarily inaccurate, simply because it must tell a story. Knowledge, plain fact, without a theme does not show well. Even wildlife documentaries require a plot. The most saleable plot is that of a species barely hanging on in the face of human exploitation, usually by logging or grazing. The logger or cowboy, or his wannabe rancher replacement, basks in his personal myth of being a Bunyon or Chisum, all the while using modern industrial tools that modify forest or develop the land with unprecedented speed. The decisions to make such modifications and the political maneuverings to bring them about are made increasingly by corporate executives who live far from the land and have no interest in wildness and no understanding of evolution.

It is in this never-never land of competitive land uses that the

wildlife biologist functions, buffeted from all sides by commercial interests, environmental groups, and the urban consumers who provide
the market for land-based resources. Amidst this, the wildlife biologist must maintain his own personal myth—that he knows what he is
doing. He envisages a process wherein habitat (that nebulous complex of food, water, and cover) is modified to benefit a certain wild
species. But at this point, he is already in trouble, for managing for
one species will certainly be management against another, so selection sets in. Some call this playing God, but it really seems to be more
of a human trait.

Even where the act of managing habitat to benefit a single species might be possible, the time frame involved in managing western
wildlands often prevents us from seeing the results of our efforts.
Regrowth of habitat happens slowly. More often than not an individual
biologist setting a project in motion will have moved on to other jobs
long before he can see the fruits of his labor or be accountable for it.
In fact, many habitat management projects might require the lifetimes
of several biologists before clear results are seen. Yet our monitoring, if done at all, uses inadequate techniques applied annually, simply to provide an illusion of doing something.

Finally, the most important information, and most difficult to
convey, is what we do not know—the black holes in the matrix of
knowledge. Gathering new information is an incremental process,
with the direction of a study implied only by past insights and guided
by available technology. Outside of our individual realm of experience are many undiscovered truths about every aspect of nature, even
about something as well studied as turkeys. If such unknowns are
too remote from our current level of awareness, we are then simply
unaware of our ignorance of them, and we have no way to point our
research in their direction. Thus top-down direction of research by
politicians or administrators may clutter the process and slow
progress. Yet administrators and politicians continue to create politically driven studies and use them to postpone decisions.

Our understanding of Merriam's turkey habitat is confounded by
uncertainties regarding the bird's origins. The evidence gives strong

support to the belief that Merriam's turkey is a recent arrival in the Southwest. It almost certainly arrived after the first humans came to the area. At present, we cannot be sure that it has been here more than about two thousand years. Several archaeologists believe that early Indians transplanted the bird, but I don't think that we need to solicit help from humans to explain the bird's arrival. It probably drifted into the western United States after habitats became more compatible with post-Pleistocene warming. The best evidence to date says it came mainly from the East, rather than from Latin America.

If this is so, Merriam's turkey was probably still expanding its range when early naturalists arrived to note its presence. We must therefore be cautious in using Arizona, New Mexico, and Colorado habitats as absolute models for Merriam's turkey habitat management. The Merriam's turkey may represent a relatively new subspecies struggling to survive in marginal range. And none of the existing forests, where we tend now to evaluate habitat selection, are necessarily similar to the forests present when Europeans arrived.

Much of our habitat research to this time has been descriptive. We know what kinds of trees are used as roosts; we have a good picture of nesting habitat; and we know where broods feed in the understory that remains. But we know little of the adaptive values of turkey behaviors associated with these habitats. Because of its late arrival and eastern affinity, we need to compare our knowledge of the Merriam's turkey with the more extensive knowledge of the eastern bird. How different is our southwestern bird in its habitat needs? Are the observed differences beneficial adaptations, or are they indicators of populations hanging on by the skin of their beaks in a peripheral and marginal landscape?

During the past decade or so, habitat has become a household word in our society, but I doubt that many who use it understand the depth of its meaning. The tropical forests of Latin America are on everyone's lips, and virtually all crises involving threatened species are recognized as results of habitat loss rather than direct exploitation of wildlife populations. Endangered taxa, such as the spotted owl, the Mt. Graham red squirrel, and the Florida panther, are used as symbols of declining habitats that are also homes for other wild species. Turkeys, too, occasionally assume this symbolic role when they happen to be the most visible or valuable (from human perspectives) species in an area. In both Arizona and Utah, Merriam's turkeys have figured in attempts to limit logging of ponderosa pine. On some National Forests in the west, turkeys are classed as Management Indicator Species (MIS) and used to assess the health of wildlife habitats. The MIS concept is based on the assumption that maintaining good habitat for a few key species will assure retention of habitats for a larger variety of species that use part or all of the same habitats. We do not, perhaps cannot, know the detailed requirements of the hundreds of wild mammals and birds (to say nothing of the invertebrates) on wildlands. We can (and to some extent do) understand the needs of a few, which are used as miner's canaries.

In understanding the detailed daily and seasonal behavior of animals in their environments, our conceptualization of habitat, while limited, has nonetheless advanced much too rapidly for either politicians or the general public to keep up. Even professional biologists find it difficult to absorb existing knowledge and an ever-widening gap exists between biologists and laymen. The gap may be too great to bridge. The average citizen, urban or rural, simply does not have the time or inclination to keep up with accumulating ecological knowledge. In fact, those who make their living directly from the land—ranchers, loggers, guides—quite often view the barrage of new biological information as a threat and are reacting more and more with resistance to science-based fact. In some cases, they are retreating into creationism and fundamental religions, because these beliefs support their anthropocentric viewpoints and economic needs better than the new ecology. In some ways, they cannot be blamed, for we are so totally deluged daily with information from the various media that even experts have trouble differentiating fact from fiction.

As ecologists, we see that humans, because of their ability to affect the planet, must become altruists. If we are to survive, we must nurture other species. This vision has occurred at a time when everyone else seems to be sliding rapidly toward a worship of the dollar and devaluation of wildness. Even as we learn more about wild species, the probability of ever being able to apply this new knowledge grows smaller, as wildlife becomes an impediment to accumulating wealth. The Merriam's turkey is not the only creature whose fate awaits the outcome of this cultural digression.

Notes

Chapter 1. Salting Tails

1. For those unacquainted with hunting systems, a permit lottery involves the hunter mailing a form by a predetermined deadline. On a given date, a drawing is held, and permits are then mailed to those chosen. Before computers became available, drawings required someone to actually reach into a barrel and pull out the hunter's "ticket." These were then individually hand-processed and mailed. The workload and expense were immense, and with the rapidly increasing number of hunters in the state after World War II, the department sought ways to avoid drawings. With computerization, of course, "drawings" are now held by allowing the computer to randomly select "winners" and mailing permits automatically. As a result, the selection of hunters by lottery is fairly easy. Virtually all big game hunters in Arizona, including turkey hunters, are now selected by lottery.

2. Steve Gallizioli worked on Gambel's quail population studies for over twenty years. His reports resulted in liberalized hunting seasons and limits for quail in Arizona. He also demonstrated the dependence of this species on winter and spring rainfall, showing that annual reproduction was triggered by the amount of green feed available in the spring.

Chapter 2. Soaring with Turkeys

1. In electrician's parlance, we wired the squibs in parallel across the two main lead wires. The main leads ran into the blind, where we tapped them on the posts of a twelve-volt battery when we wanted spark. Even with the wires incorrectly connected, it seems to me that they should have either failed to fire or fired instantaneously. I have never found an explanation for the sequential explosions.

Chapter 3. The Object of Our Obsession

1. I'd like to express this better, but I don't know how. As I say, books are

written on the subject, and even today, various creatures are classified and reclassified, sometimes elevated to the rank of species, sometimes reduced to the lower category of subspecies. Bird taxonomists seem especially bad about changing things around. For the present, approach it intuitively: lions are different species from tigers. Turkeys are different species from pheasants or grouse. Merriam's turkeys are the same species as wild turkeys in Pennsylvania, Florida, or Texas, but they are just different enough in color and, perhaps, size, to be considered unique.

2. Gould's turkey extends into southwestern New Mexico and southeastern Arizona. The dividing line between the ranges of the two subspecies is still a matter of conjecture.

3. These first birds seen in Europe may have already been modified from wild stock by way of selective breeding, intentional or otherwise. This may have further complicated classification of other subspecies as specimens of wild birds from other parts of the continent began to arrive.

4. Samuel Woodhouse, in 1853, however, did not think that the turkeys around Santa Fe looked any different than those further east. Antoine Leroux informed him that the birds along the Gila were lighter. Extirpation and restoration of turkeys since that time has mixed the population genes, so we'll never know what kind of variation actually existed through the original southwestern populations.

Chapter 6. If We Could Talk to the Animals

1. Timber management terminology is a specialty of its own and too complex to cover in this book. Selective cutting, developed by early forest scientist Gus Pearson at Fort Valley, near Flagstaff, took only a few older trees at widely scattered sites through the forest. It was intended to allow logging without serious effects on the structure of the forest. Most other forms of logging create either large, treeless openings or extensive stands of scattered, small trees. These forms of logging generate a neat, undifferentiated forest. They tend to make wildlife biologists nervous.

Chapter 8. Wings and Prayers

1. I don't think any of us would have guessed where this would lead in a short thirty years. Today several individuals in Montana and Wyoming actually make a fair percentage of their living locating wildlife by radio for various agencies. These people fly aircraft fitted with satellite positioning equipment that feeds directly into laptop computers, providing automatically recorded locations. Satellites are actually tracking a few larger species, such as caribou and whales. Our

challenge today seems not to be gathering information about animals, but rather keeping the animals around, while we try to get a materialistic public to care whether wildlife exists at all.

Chapter 9. The Best Laid Plans of Men and Turkeys

1. These so-called "treatments" were actually a wide variety of forms of timber clearing and thinning done on areas of two hundred to five hundred acres. This created a diverse mosaic of openings, thinnings, and unmodified forest in a relatively small area. It seemed an ideal place to study habitat selection by turkeys.

Chapter 10. Of Turkeys and Hunters

1. Ah yes, even those camouflage-clad gents with their four-wheel drive pickups and arrays of turkey calls and decoys have social constraints.

Suggested Additional Reading

For the latest summary of technical information on all aspects of the wild turkey, *The Wild Turkey: Biology and Management* (1992), edited by James G. Dickson, is excellent. It covers all but the very latest information on wild turkey behavior and taxonomy, and discusses habitat requirements of each subspecies. If you want the very latest research, the National Wild Turkey Federation has all eight of the National Wild Turkey Symposia proceedings, along with other publications, available on a single CD-ROM. A wonderfully scholarly book is *The Wild Turkey: Its History and Domestication* (1966), by A. W. Schorger. The coverage of early technical literature, history, and archaeology is complete to its time. For more specific coverage of Merriam's turkey history, try to find J. Stokely Ligon's 1948 book *History and Management of Merriam's Wild Turkey.* This was published by the University of New Mexico Press and is long out of print. For just fun reading, Joe Hutto's *Illumination in the Flatwoods* (1995) tells a wonderful story of turkeys imprinted on an interested layman. Hutto shows us that even turkeys can teach us a lot.

About the Author

Harley Shaw grew up mainly in Phoenix, Arizona, although it was a winter in eastern Oklahoma after World War II, when he was nine years old, that sparked his interest in the outdoors. He found a new freedom in wandering the pastures and wooded hills and fishing along Little Sallisaw Creek. Hunting and fishing became a passion with him in his teens and early adulthood, which led him to study wildlife management at the University of Arizona, where he graduated with honors in 1960. While attending the University, he worked for four summers with the Arizona Game and Fish Department, starting as a development laborer and graduating to banding studies of mourning doves, white-winged doves, and Gambel's quail. He also spent one year working with the late Lyle Sowls on javelina.

Mr. Shaw went on to the University of Idaho and completed a master of science in wildlife management in 1963. He started on a Ph.D. at Washington State University, but a family illness required that he seek gainful employment. He returned to the Arizona Game and Fish Department and took over a mule deer study on the Three Bar Wildlife Area. When turkey research was proposed in northern Arizona, he requested to be transferred to that project. He later worked on puma and desert bighorn sheep, retiring from the department in 1990.

Since that time, he has taken on a variety of consulting projects, including turkey habitat assessments in Utah and Arizona, a pronghorn transplant feasibility study at Joshua Tree National Park, and an assessment of the effects of predator control on Arizona pronghorn. He also helped design a puma monitoring plan for Saguaro National Park. He carried out an independent study of vegetation change in northern Arizona and has continued to write on a variety of subjects. His earlier book, *Soul Among Lions,* was originally published in 1991 by Johnson Books and reissued by the University of Arizona Press in 2000. He now lives with his wife, Patty Woodruff, in Hillsboro, New Mexico.